PRAISE FOR KEEP MOVING FORWARD

The beauty of Melony Brown's writing is not simply in her ability to craft story and hope in a meaningful way, but how the substance of her own life is woven into her work. Every word is an extension of the victory she's lived and an invitation to find life even in the most unexpected places. *Keep Moving Forward* is honest, inspirational, and life changing. If you're going to trust a guide on how to overcome and flourish, I recommend following one of the few who has actually done it. I can't recommend this book enough.

Phil Manginelli

Lead Pastor at The Square Church

Have you experienced unusual life circumstances? Are you struggling to move beyond the pain? *Keep Moving Forward* is unique in structure, approach, and power but that's precisely what you need. Like having a guide lead you out of the dark woods where you have landed, this book will equip you and shine a light on your path forward.

Lori Stanley Roeleveld

Coach, speaker, and award-winning author of *Graceful Influence: Making a Lasting Impact through Lessons from Women of the Bible*

D1157912

Reading a new book is like being introduced to a new acquaintance; it often takes only a few pages to know whether you'll become fast friends. In *Keep Moving Forward*, Melony Brown's second volume in her Journey On! series, you'll meet an experienced trail guide whose empathetic voice, can-do spirit and interactive survival guide provides just the trusted companionship you need as you confront life's challenges head-on. Through targeted questions, compelling visuals, scriptural principles, and uplifting stories of overcomers, *Keep Moving Forward* will teach you to do exactly that.

Maggie Wallem Rowe

Dramatist, speaker, and author of *This Life We Share: 52 Reflections on Journeying Well with God and Others*

In *Keep Moving Forward*, Melony Brown weaves God's Word and personal stories seamlessly throughout the book to keep us moving forward in our spiritual walk with the Lord. You'll delve into such topics as trusting God, growing and thriving, refining fires, facing our fears, and much more. My favorite reminder? Words from Moses, recorded in Deuteronomy: "The LORD your God, who is going before you, will fight for you." Join Melony in this powerful, new resource. Keep moving forward while hanging on to God's Word and His promises!

Julie Lavender

Author of the best-selling book, *Children's Bible Stories for Bedtime,* and the award-winning book, *365 Ways to Love Your Child: Turning Little Moments into Lasting Memories*

KEEP MOVING
FORWARD

An Interactive Survival Guide
for Overcoming & Thriving

Journey On!
SERIES
BOOK 2

Seek to grow through every challenge, knowing it all leads to Heaven!

Melony Brown

2 Cor. 3:18

MELONY BROWN

FICTION HOUSE
PRESS

Brown, Melony, author

Keep Moving Forward: An Interactive Survival Guide for Overcoming & Thriving

Includes biographical references.

ISBN 979-8-9866245-2-5   ISBN 979-8-9866245-3-2 (eBook)

Cover design and interior formatting by *Hannah Linder Designs*

Author photo by Alicia Dixon Photography © 2023. All rights reserved.

Printed in the United States of America

To my son, Ashton—
Challenges haven't stopped you. They gifted you your work
ethic, grit, and perseverance.
So incredibly proud of you.

CONTENTS

RESTED, RECHARGED & READY!

there ain't no journey what don't change you some.1

—author David Mitchell

A n elderly gentleman, hunched over a plate of hors d'oeuvres and a generous slice of wedding cake, sat at the farthest corner of the reception hall. I wandered over and asked if I could join him. His casual nod welcomed me. Followed by a smile and a Texas-sized mustache with a curl on each end. "Beautiful day for a wedding," I said.

"Chit-chat lacks teeth, young lady. Offer me something meaty to chew on," he teased. Before I could respond, he launched into his life story. Sometime later, he encouraged me to enlighten him with mine. Sharing our scars, hope, struggles, laughter, and joy connected us. "You've overcome some incredibly difficult challenges, Hugh. You have an amazing attitude," I said.

Hugh's blue eyes met mine, then darted away. "Thank you kindly. When you trust God's plan for your life, challenges are just cleverly disguised opportunities to grow." He chuckled before continuing. "I wasn't about to waste those opportunities. Growth was hard but worth it. I bet you could say the same."

A call to send the bride and groom off on their honeymoon ended our conversation. Sadly, I couldn't find Hugh before we headed home.

So, wherever you are Hugh, thank you for the meaty conversation, and yes, trusting God during my challenges positively impacted my life in ways I could have never imagined. I'm so grateful.

LIFE IS FULL OF CHALLENGES

Since parting ways in *Challenges Won't Stop Me,* a 'cleverly disguised opportunity' intersected my path, reminding me of Hugh's words. Once again, God invited me to trust His plan. While I could share the positive outcomes of my latest challenge, it's time to keep moving forward!

It's a fortuitous blessing to have a parking lot located near our starting place for the second half of our journey. I arrived at the parking lot early, giddy with excitement. I've been looking forward to reconnecting with those who journeyed with me in *Challenges Won't Stop Me* and meeting new friends here in *Keep Moving Forward*. While I waited for everyone to arrive, I observed quite a few hikers entering and leaving the trail. What struck me most were the hikers who jumped out of their cars and headed into the woods unprepared. No backpack. No water. No gear. Perhaps they believed they wouldn't encounter any challenges while hiking the trails.

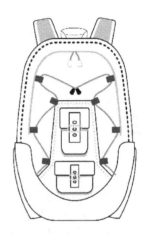

I know, and I bet you've lived enough life to know, life is full of challenges. You're either exiting a challenge, in the middle of one, or a new challenge is just around the corner. We cannot avoid challenges, but we can be prepared for them. The best chance of fighting to overcome life's tough challenges starts with being prepared.

Just as I finished my snack, a group of weary hikers emerged from the trails, searching for a water fountain. No germ-infested water fountains in this parking lot. I offered each hiker a cold bottle of water and an invitation to join us for the second half of our journey. Their hesitant responses weren't surprising.

Several vehicles arrived, diverting my attention. Multiple friends from *Challenges Won't Stop Me* emerged from a two-door car, looking like a group of jovial circus clowns that somehow all fit in a tiny car. Their laughter carried across the parking lot, turning the heads of the unprepared hikers. As my friends drifted toward our designated meeting spot, I noticed the hikers merging into the group. Curiosity was written across their faces.

A DANGEROUS PATH

While describing how God lifted her out of a five-year long abusive relationship, Kristen pulled a rope out of her backpack. A tall girl asked her how a rope helped. "Just like a rope, my ex-boyfriend was constantly oppositional and resisted working toward peace. He would pull my hair and drag me back to the bedroom to abuse me. But God extended His hand and lifted me toward Him. I'm healing. Consistently using my essential gear equips me. I won't make those same mistakes again," Kristen replied.

Near the only patch of grass, Rosalyn looked at a map with one of the hikers, tracing the length of the next part of our journey. After tucking the map into a side pocket, she searched inside her backpack and pulled out her Bible. "For many years, bad choices led me down a dangerous path," Rosalyn explained. "I saw how characters in Bible stories chose dangerous paths, which then led to negative outcomes. Their stories convinced me. I didn't want my story to end like theirs. I am eager to study God's Word because it guides me to make better choices. My Bible is my map, directing me to good paths on my life journey."

Matthew jogged toward me with a huge smile on his face. "Ask me to give you a status update." Before I could respond, he said, "During the last few months, my girlfriend and I fought every day. Even though I loved her, I believed I needed to break up. Before I did, I remembered my essential gear and pulled out my binoculars. I praised God for allowing our paths to cross. I thanked Him for all her wonderful traits and how she shows her love. It totally changed my perspective. I proposed last week. She said yes!"

INVITE GOD TO BE YOUR MASTER NAVIGATOR

A buzz of excitement spread throughout the parking lot. One of the young men who'd come unprepared for his hike whistled. The shrill noise caused everyone to stop talking and turn to him. "Sorry," he said. "I'm not part of your group, but I gotta know about this lingo you're using. Ropes are more than ropes. Bibles are maps. And binoculars saved a relationship. What am I missing?"

Justin laughed. "I hadn't thought of the essential gear having its own lingo, but it does. We took a journey together to learn how to be prepared for the challenges of life. First and foremost, you need to invite God to be your Master Navigator. And then learn about the essential gear. God's truth will prepare you for whatever challenge dares to cross your path."

Hearing their stories touched me, but not only me. These stories were also clearly impacting the weary hikers. "Anyone else have a story?" I asked.

LaDonna spoke up. "Periods of dark depression have challenged me my whole life. I learned during the first half of our journey that the light of Jesus dispels the darkness and illu-  minates potential dangers. A flashlight reminds me of how powerful His light is." She held up her flashlight. "Sev- eral weeks ago, I wanted to end my darkness. To end my life. Instead of taking a bottle of pills, I recon- nected with God and asked Him to shine the brightest light into my pain." She slowly made eye contact with each person in the group. "And He did!" Cheers erupted.

Benjamin walked across the circle to LaDonna and gave her a high- five. "God is so good! I see His light in your eyes!" He looked around the group and said, "Since we parted ways, life has been rough. My wife of thirty years fought hard to beat ovarian cancer. Unfortunately, it took her life. I felt lost without her. My grief has been great."

Benjamin paused a moment before continuing, "Initially, I blamed God. My so-called friends were happy to join in my rantings. When they began encouraging me to numb my pain with substances and casual sex, I realized I was seeking comfort and refuge in the world's tent. I found my multi-purpose tool and prayed for God to forgive my hard heart and to help me grieve. Then I ran back to God's tent. He comforted me. I still miss my precious wife, but God's love has surrounded me. And I'm experiencing joy again."

I couldn't hold back my tears any longer. "May God be praised!

Some might think having all those pieces of essential gear in your back-pack would make it heavy and burdensome. But I'd argue this gear makes everything lighter. Much lighter. Especially when it is consistently used as each of your stories demonstrate. When we invite God to navigate our journey, He takes the burden of our challenges off us and puts it on Him. We weren't meant to carry those burdens. May these stories build our faith and trust in God."

The tall girl asked if she could join us. "You bet! Anyone else?" I was overjoyed to see several of the weary hikers wander to the back of my Jeep and grab backpacks filled with essential gear. "Looks like everyone is prepared for the journey ahead, so let's go!"

REVEAL TRUTHS THAT WILL STRENGTHEN YOU

Whether you were a part of the journey in *Challenges Won't Stop Me*, or you're joining us now in *Keep Moving Forward*, welcome! I'm so grateful you've chosen to create a survival guide to fight to overcome the challenges of life and thrive! Permit me to share a few ways to gain the most benefits from reading this book.

First and foremost, this isn't a quick read. I wrote this survival guide to be interactive, which takes time. But the payoff is worth your investment. Actively participate by writing notes and observations in the margins.

Use colored pencils or crayons to color the black and white visual images of the expected encounters you'll see at each mile marker and throughout the book. You may be thinking, "Nah. I'll pass on the coloring part." Please don't! Coloring engages the part of your brain that processes what you're learning. My friends, Karen and Shanna, agree coloring the visual images in *Challenges Won't Stop Me* helped them remember what each piece of essential gear represents. Time spent reflecting on and then answering the questions will be invaluable.

Your answers will often reveal truths that will strengthen you for the rest of your journey. Please don't skip over the questions.

As we journey together, I will share Bible verses which will connect with the topic presented. Even if you've read the verses many times, please read them again. God may be shedding fresh insight that you will need as you fight to overcome this challenge. A fight verse is your 'go-to' verse any time a tough challenge intersects your path. This verse serves many purposes. It may encourage you. Or make you feel less anxious. Or fill you with courage and strength. Maybe it reminds you to put your armor on. Or prompts you to draw near to God as He fights for you. Whatever purpose it serves, you need one!

If you have a fight verse, please write it below. If you don't have one, pick a specific color of highlighter to highlight verses that speak to you as you are creating your survival guide. Just before we part ways at the end of this book, I'll ask you to write your fight verse in several places.

INVITE YOU INTO A DEEPER RELATIONSHIP WITH GOD

Since 2013, I've been blessed to interview over 150 courageous women who've fought to overcome one or more of life's tough challenges. I will share excerpts from some of those overcomer interviews to illustrate how the expected encounters invite you into a deeper relationship with God and help you grow.

If you connect with a particular overcomer's story, the tiny capital letter to the right of each overcomer's name corresponds with the letters in the 'Appendix of Overcomer Stories' at the back of this book. On the appendix page, you'll find the overcomer's first name, the title of her story, the date her story was published, and the word *Story* or *Podcast*. Once you locate the overcomer you'd like to know more about, go to www.melonybrown.com. Then, click on the *Stories tab* and type the name of her story in the search bar, or click on the *Podcast tab* and scroll to the correct season and episode number. *Please note that on 12/21/22, I changed the name of my podcast from *Zigzag & 1* (seasons 1-4) to *Challenges Won't Stop Me* (season 5 and beyond).

Because we will continue to use the essential gear from *Challenges Won't Stop Me* throughout the second half of our journey, let's create an easy reference for each piece of gear and its purpose.

Fill in the following blanks with the seven pieces of essential gear. You may refer to your notes in *Challenges Won't Stop Me* or reread the previous two sections, LIFE IS FULL OF CHALLENGES and INVITE GOD TO BE YOUR MASTER NAVIGATOR.

- A road _____ of God's Word guides and directs your path during the smooth sailing times and challenging times.
- A pair of _____ invites you to praise and worship God, moving your focus from the struggles ten feet in front of you to fixing your eyes on Him.
- God's _____ offers you true safety, protection, and refuge when life's challenges overwhelm.
- The _____ provides a deep connection with God. Prayer serves multiple purposes.
- The _____ lifts you to God when you are being dragged or facing opposition/resistance.
- A _____ gives you a place to record your journey, remember what you're learning, and an opportunity to see your growth.

- A _____ dispels the darkness and
  illuminates potential dangers in your path.

Answers on page 209.

Make this an easy reference by writing ESSENTIAL GEAR on the edge of a sticky note and adding it to the side of this page.

God gave us these pieces of essential gear to draw us closer to Him and to equip and empower us to fight to overcome life's tough challenges. Remember, Satan doesn't care if you *possess* the pieces of essential gear. But he IS significantly threatened if you consistently *use* them to prepare for whatever challenges intersect your path in the future.

Please highlight the last two sentences.

In the space below, describe your commitment to consistently using your essential gear.

AN UNUSUAL PLACE

A parking lot is an unusual place to start a book about moving forward. Please stay with me. Starting here will make sense soon. When we park our vehicle in a parking lot, we stop or settle for a considerable period. Sometimes the same can be said of us, especially when difficult challenges intersect our path or when they linger way too long.

In the preceding paragraph, please double underline *stop or settle* and *for a considerable period*.

Merriam-Webster defines *stop* as "to hinder or prevent the passage of; to get in the way of; to close or block off; to make impassable; to keep from carrying out a proposed action; to cause to cease; to discontinue; to come to an end; to break one's journey." *Settle* is defined as "to cause to pack down; to establish or secure permanently; to come to rest; to sink gradually."

Do any of the definitions for *stop* or *settle* resonate with you? If so, highlight them.

Think of a time when you *stopped* or *settled* for a considerable period. Describe the circumstances of the challenge you were facing. What compelled you to start again? Was it easy or difficult to get going again?

Stopping to rest or recuperate is sometimes necessary. However, we must consider that resting can become a slippery slope. Sometimes, settling for a considerable period gets comfortable and turns into a permanent situation. The slippery slope looks like this: stopping too long slides into settling, and then, settling often slides into getting stuck. *Merriam-Webster* defines *stuck* as "to become blocked, wedged, or jammed; to be unable to proceed."

ON YOUR WAY NOW

In Deuteronomy chapter one, the generation of Israelites born during the forty-year journey in the wilderness had been camping at the base of Mount Horeb. Concerned they had gotten too comfortable (settled), Moses recounted all the ways God protected them and fought for them, so that they could courageously enter the Promised Land. He urged the people to keep moving forward and take possession of God's promise.

On the plains of Moab before the Israelites crossed the Jordan River and entered the Promised Land, Moses reiterated what God commanded: "Back at Horeb, GOD, our God, spoke to us: 'You've stayed long enough at this mountain. On your way now. Get moving. Head for the Amorite hills, wherever people are living in the Arabah, the mountains, the foothills, the Negev, the seashore—the Canaanite country and the Lebanon all the way to the big river, the Euphrates. Look, I've given you this land. Now go in and take it. It's the land GOD promised to give your ancestors Abraham, Isaac, and Jacob and their children after them'" (Deuteronomy 1:6-8, MSG).

See anything about not *settling*? About not getting *stuck*? Please highlight *you've stayed long enough at this mountain, on your way now,* and *get moving.*

These phrases urged the first generation of Israelites to keep moving forward. The call to action in Moses' speech—Look, I've given you this land. Now go in and take it—precedes Moses reminding the current generation of Israelites of several key events during their forty-year journey in the wilderness.

Double underline Moses' call to action.

In the following paragraph, please highlight the challenges the ten spies perceived.

Moses reminded the Israelites of the first time they reached the Promised Land. Twelve spies were sent to assess Canaan. Upon their return, ten of the spies reported, "it does flow with milk and honey ... But the people who are there are powerful, and the cities are fortified and very large ... We can't attack these people; they are stronger than we are" (Numbers 13:27-28, 31).

Suppose the ten spies had chosen to use their binoculars instead of focusing on the challenges ten feet in front of them. The challenges might not have changed, but their perspective about who would help them overcome those challenges likely would have changed.

While reading Joshua and Caleb's assessment of the land, use a different color highlighter to mark their perspective of the challenges.

Joshua and Caleb said, "The land we passed through and explored is exceedingly good. If the LORD is pleased with us, he will lead us into that land, a land flowing with milk and honey, and will give it to us. Only do not rebel against the LORD. And do not be afraid of the people of the land, because we will devour them. Their protection is gone, but the LORD is with us. Do not be afraid of them" (Numbers 14:7-9).

Describe Joshua and Caleb's focus and trust.

Please highlight *the LORD is with us.*

The ten spies stirred up grumbling among the Israelites, which angered God. Those who did not trust God to fight for them were struck down and died of a plague. In contrast, God commended Joshua and Caleb's faithfulness and spared their lives. This was the moment the Israelites learned they would wander in the wilderness for forty years: "one year for each of the days you explored the land ..." (Numbers 14:34).

CHOOSE TO REMEMBER GOD'S PROVISION AND PROTECTION

The Israelites were at the edge of the Promised Land a second time. This time they were preparing to take possession of it. Would the Israelites choose to remember the giants who were seen in the Promised Land all those years ago? Or would they remember God's provision and protection during their forty years of wandering? If they remembered the giants, the Israelites would once again get stuck.

As Moses recounted their time in the wilderness, he pointed out how he told them 'to not be afraid,' 'to not be discouraged,' and 'to not be terrified' (Deuteronomy 1:17, 1:21, 1:29, 3:2, and 3:22). Perhaps these words weren't enough to convince the first generation of Israelites to keep moving forward.

So, Moses reminded them, "The LORD your God, who is going before you, will fight for you, as he did for you in Egypt, before your very eyes, and in the wilderness. There you saw how the LORD your God carried you, as a father carries his son, all the way you went until you reached this place" (Deuteronomy 1:30-31).

Please highlight *The LORD your God, who is going before you, will fight for you.* **Double underline** *will fight for you.*

Near the end of his sermon, Moses described how God fought for this generation of Israelites against the armies of Sihon king of Heshbon and Og king of Bashan. Then Moses commanded Joshua, "You have seen with your own eyes all that the LORD has done to these two kings.

The LORD will do the same to all the kingdoms over there where you are going. Do not be afraid of them; the LORD your God himself will fight for you" (Deuteronomy 3:21-22).

Please highlight *the LORD your God himself will fight for you.* **Double underline** *will fight for you.*

Describe how knowing God fights for you compels you to trust Him to 'do it again.' How does knowing this help you to keep moving forward?

By reminding the Israelites God would fight for them now as He had done before, Moses hoped to instill in them that God could do it again. Their 'challenges won't stop us' mindset was not based on what they had done. Rather, it was based on what God had done. If God provided for and protected them before, He could do it again. Their mindset was not based on their grit or determination or lack of fear but on God filling them with courage and faith in Him. This mindset would fortify the Israelites, enabling them to keep moving forward, no matter what challenge lay ahead.

TRAIL ETIQUETTE & INSTRUCTIONS

I mentioned in *Challenges Won't Stop Me* that our journey isn't a thru-hike. We collected our essential gear as we hiked the first eight miles of a sixteen-mile journey. We'll hike the remaining eight miles in this book. Before we head out, I offer this warning: these eight miles will be more challenging than the first eight. The challenges we faced in *Chal-*

lenges Won't Stop Me were the unexpected challenges of life. We learned the benefits of being prepared for them. Additionally, our gear proved to be essential *and* effective when fighting to overcome life's challenges.

While we can anticipate and prepare for these expected encounters, you might find yourself feeling overwhelmed and decide giving up is the better option than continuing to fight. Don't let fear or discouragement stop you, make you settle, or cause you to get stuck. To remind you God is fighting with you and for you, write Deuteronomy 1:30-31 and 3:21-22 from the CHOOSE TO REMEMBER GOD'S PROVISION AND PROTECTION section in your travel log. Say these verses out loud every time defeat, discouragement, or overwhelm creeps in. Remember, God's Word is a powerful offensive weapon when the enemy attacks.

Be of good cheer! Several miles in *Keep Moving Forward* include expected encounters that will nourish you, help you grow, bless you, and fuel you to keep moving forward. Thank goodness God knows we need good encounters mixed in with our weeks/months/years of tough encounters. Before we hit the trail, please read the Trail Etiquette & Instructions sign.

TRAIL ETIQUETTE & INSTRUCTIONS

- SAY HELLO AS YOU PASS OTHERS ON THE TRAIL.
  Offer friendship and support to others who are struggling.

- MINIMIZE DISTRACTIONS.
  Take a break from technology. Let your phone store voicemails, texts, and emails until you're ready to check them.

- COLOR THE VISUAL IMAGES AND MAKE CONNECTIONS.
  Connecting the gear to visual images improves retention.

- ANSWER QUESTIONS, HIGHLIGHT & UNDERLINE.
  Actively engage to create a meaningful survival guide.

- MAINTAIN YOUR CHALLENGES WON'T STOP ME MINDSET.
  When you face unexpected turns or expected encounters, trust that God is with you and He fights for you.

Let's do a quick status check. Are you rested? Recharged? Is your essential gear packed? Is your mindset one of challenges won't stop me? Great! You'll need that mindset for those expected encounters just around the corner.

Do not fear. Do not be afraid. Instead, be strong and courageous! I believe God is going before us and navigating our path. He will fight for us. Are you ready? Let's journey on!

… we must keep moving. If you can't fly, run; if you can't run, walk; if you can't walk, crawl;

but by all means keep moving.2

—an excerpt from a speech Martin Luther King, Jr. delivered at Spelman College

mile 09

Will You Trust Your Connection to God?

The ultimate test of faith is not how loudly you praise God in happy times
but how deeply you trust him in dark times.1
—Rick Warren, pastor and author

Despite that summer day occurring forty years ago, vivid details remain in my memory. The neighborhood crew rose early to play kickball in the cul-de-sac. In less than an hour, the unrelenting heat wave depleted our energy and enthusiasm. Jonathan suggested we play in the creek to cool off, which meant catching copperhead snakes. His suggestion was immediately shot down. Three trips through the sprinklers at my house offered little relief.

Now what? It was 10:30 in the morning, and we'd already crossed into the land of boredom. The neighborhood bully asked, "What's there to do?" The youngest of our ragtag group, Scott, suggested we play *Trust Fall*. None of us were familiar with that game, but an opportunity to escape the oppressive heat wooed us inside his air-conditioned house. His mom looked up from her work and waved as the seven of us headed down the steps to their basement.

Scott began delegating tasks while explaining the rules for *Trust Fall*. "When it's your turn, face my dad's workbench and then fall backward. The rest of us will catch you," he said. My stomach lurched. *While these kids were fun to hang out with, did I trust them to catch me?*

Lauren volunteered to go first. After she climbed up on the table, Scott asked her, "Do you trust us to catch your fall?" Lauren shouted, "Yes!" Three of us clasped arms with the three kids across from us, creating a basket in which to catch her. "Ok, Go!" Scott said. Lauren fell back. The six of us caught her in our arms. Same scenario for the next kid. And the next.

When Demetrius said it was his turn, each set of eyes darted to the ones across the way. Fear set in quicker than a dog snatching a morsel of food as it's falling to the floor. You see, Demetrius wasn't fat. He was just a stocky guy. The makeshift table wobbled when he climbed up on it. "I'm ready. Ask the question." Scott hesitated, looking at each of us before saying, "Do you trust us to catch your fall?" Demetrius laughed and fell back before Scott could say, "Ok, Go!"

My memory still processes that moment in slow motion. Scott and Jonathan's arms were the only ones linked. Unfortunately, their efforts weren't enough to catch his fall. Demetrius' head hit the concrete floor with an audible thud.

No surprise that Scott's mom heard the commotion. She opened the door and yelled, "What was that noise?" We looked at one another. Our pre-fall fear escalated to panic. Scott yelled, "Demetrius fell. Don't worry, Mom. I'm helping him up." Knowing his mom would be coming down to the basement to investigate and scold us, the rest of us raced out the garage door.

TRUSTED US TO CATCH HIM

Demetrius' family moved into the neighborhood five years before the *Trust Fall* incident. When we learned his dad worked at Coke and brought home an endless supply of Cokes each day, there was no question about whether he could hang out with us. Cokes aside, Demetrius was an interesting kid.

That summer day, he trusted us to catch him. Would we have caught Demetrius' fall if we'd linked arms in time? Maybe. I just can't be certain. We were mere humans. Skinny ones at that. In case you're wondering, Demetrius suffered a nasty concussion and couldn't hang out with us for six weeks. We were too scared to visit him, fearing he would spill the beans about which of us didn't catch his fall.

A few days before Demetrius' six weeks of recovery ended, we noticed a moving truck in his driveway. Its distinct grumble woke me two days later. I quickly changed out of my pajamas and ran to his house. Not apologizing to Demetrius had eaten me up.

His dad greeted me just outside their garage doors. "Hi, Mel. Here to say bye to Demetrius?" I couldn't hold my anxious thoughts in any longer. "No. sir. I came to apologize. I let Demetrius down by not catching him when he fell. I didn't want him leaving without telling him I'm sorry."

He pointed up to Demetrius' window. "Head up to his room. He'll be glad to see you." Just as I began walking away, Demetrius' dad said, "Mel, the only person we can trust one hundred percent of the time is God."

I turned back. "Thank you, sir. I really needed to hear that."

ONLY ONE WE CAN TRUST

However much we trust our spouse, our friends, and our parents, Demetrius' dad was correct. God IS the only One we can trust one hundred percent of the time.

Highlight the previous sentence. Describe why you agree or disagree.

The *Trust Fall* game lost its allure after 'the Demetrius incident.' I'm grateful he accepted my apology. Thanking me for being his friend about undid me. Even though he admitted he fell before we were ready, I carried the shame of not catching him long after his moving van faded in the distance. I carried his dad's words too. They rolled around in my head for years.

Trusting God wasn't a specific sermon topic when my mom and I began going to church. But the idea of trusting God was almost always connected to other topics, like drawing near to God, praying for someone's healing, asking for guidance or direction, and believing He was working even though we can't always see it. I concluded our connection to God fortifies our trust in Him.

WON'T BECOME UNATTACHED

As we transition from the first half of our survival guide to the second, I chose a carabiner to represent both a piece of gear and an expected encounter. Carabiners are a metal loop with a spring-loaded gate used to connect components quickly and reversibly in a safety-critical system. The locking mechanism on a carabiner is critical. With this part engaged, ropes, additional carabiners, and anchors can be securely connected. This little piece of gear is assurance that you won't become unattached.

Rock climbers, hikers, those who explore caves, window cleaners, those who pilot hot air balloons, and white-water rescuers use carabiners to connect to a safety point. Knowing a safety system is in place allows the person to enjoy the activity or complete the task. Therefore, a visual image of a carabiner will represent our connection to God, the One whom we can trust one hundred percent of the time.

Look at the visual image of the carabiner again and take note of the long section opposite the locking mechanism. This long section, called the spine, is the strongest part of the carabiner. Carabiners connected at the spine can withstand the constant pull of a rope that connects a climber to an anchor or to the belay person.

The spine of the carabiner reminds me of the tensile strength of rope from mile 02 in *Challenges Won't Stop Me*. Tensile strength is the greatest stress a substance can bear without tearing apart. Isn't it interesting that ropes and carabiners are used together?

A rope's three purposes are resistance/opposition, dragging, and lifting. A carabiner's purpose is to connect components securely. Describe how using a rope and a carabiner together would build your faith and trust during a difficult challenge.

A GREAT DEAL OF TRUST

Knowing we'd be passing by a rock suitable for climbing, I invited two experienced climbers to meet us. They'll be spotting us on a rock climb. Wait, what? Perhaps, like me, butterflies are already flying at warp speed in your stomach. I'll admit I'm not a fan of heights. And rock climbing is definitely outside my comfort zone. You may be thinking, "Then why did you schedule this adventure?" The answer is simple: active engagement is the best way to learn!

'Going solo' is not recommended for novices. Knowing this, I invited Connie and Mike, who are experienced climbers, to spot us. The person who spots you while you are rock climbing is called a belayer. Because your life is literally in their hands, a great deal of trust is placed in your belayer.

NEVER TAKING HIS EYES OFF YOU

Are you ready? I am. Let's go! Connie and Mike brought the gear we'll need: carabiners, ropes, climbing shoes, helmets, chalk pouches with chalk, and harnesses.

As we wait for our turn to climb, you express how high and intimidating the rock is. A few of the others have struggled to make it to the top, and you share how afraid you are. You wipe your sweaty palms on your pants. Then, you look at me and say, "I committed to reading your book, not putting my life in a stranger's hands! I shouldn't have agreed to do this. I could fall and be seriously injured."

"Yes, you could," I respond. "However, Connie and Mike are very safety conscious and are committed to making this a meaningful experience. Please don't quit now. You can conquer this. I believe in you." You take a couple of deep breaths and agree to give it your best effort.

Connie calls out your name. It's your turn. You move to the spot at the base of the rock wall where you will start your climb. She performs a safety check to confirm your harness, carabiners, and ropes are secure. Connie assumes her belayer position and signals that you may begin climbing. As you ascend the rock wall, she extends the rope, allowing you to climb higher. Her only job is to spot you during your climb. Even though you can't see her, Connie never takes her eyes off you.

About a third of the way up, you encounter a ledge too small for your foot. Connie shouts out an alternate place for your right foot. Just what you needed: guidance. You adjust and keep going. After a few minutes, you stop climbing. What's wrong? Connie reacts by shouting words of encouragement. What you don't see is that she's exerting tension on the rope to counterbalance you should you fall. You shout, "I feel like I'm going to fall!" Connie shouts back, "Trust me. You can do this!"

After a few starts and stops, you reach the top. I'm so excited for you. You didn't let this challenge stop you! Connie helps you slowly walk down the rock wall. After shedding your gear, you stare at the top of the rock wall. A big smile crosses your face. Your first climb is a success! Connie snaps a few pictures to remind you of your accomplishment.

Review your rock-climbing adventure. Highlight the parts that required trust.

Your belayer never took her eyes off you. Neither does God. God never takes His eyes off you, especially not when you're facing challenges. Describe how knowing this impacts you.

TRUST HIM IN THE DARK

The smiles I see as we say good-bye to Connie and Mike confirm our rock-climbing adventure was time well spent. Now, we must keep moving forward on our journey!

Rick Warren's quote at the beginning of this mile reflects what theologian Charles Spurgeon taught: "To trust God in the light is nothing but to trust him in the dark—that is faith." [2] Spurgeon's words invite reflection. Do you trust God in the dark? Or only in the light?

Let's look at the definition of *trust* before you answer. *Merriam-Webster* defines *trust* as "assured reliance on the character, ability, strength, or truth of someone or something; to place confidence in; rely on; to hope or expect confidently; to depend."

Considering the definition for *trust*, let's answer these questions: Do you trust God in the dark places of your life?

Or do you only trust Him in the light places?

Highlight the definitions for *trust* that accurately capture your trust in God.

If you don't trust God, underline any parts of the definition for *trust* that you want/need to be true so you can build trust in God.

 When I'm studying God's Word and a verse stands out, I also read it in the Amplified Bible. Years ago, I noticed the word *trust* in the Amplified Bible was followed by "lean on, rely on, and be confident in." The amplifications expanded my understanding, so I searched biblegateway.com to find all the verses that amplified the word *trust*. I wrote the following verses in my travel log, creating reminders for those times when trusting God during a challenge takes everything in me.

Please go to biblegateway.com and scroll until you find the Amplified Bible, Classic Edition (AMPC). Write each verse with its amplifications below.

Psalm 22:4-5

Psalm 25:2

Psalm 26:1

Psalm 28:7

Psalm 31:6-8

Psalm 31:14

Psalm 32:10

Psalm 55:23

Psalm 56:3-4

Psalm 62:8

Psalm 91:2

Psalm 115:9

Psalm 119:42

Proverbs 3:5-6

Reread each verse and highlight the outcomes of *trusting* (leaning on, relying on, and being confident in) God.

Put a check mark beside the highlighted outcomes you need most in your current challenge.

Please write TRUST GOD on the edge of a colored sticky note and add it to the edge of this page for easy reference.

DECIDE TO TRUST GOD

Throughout my life, I've noticed each time a challenge intersected my path, I had to decide whether I would trust God. When I chose to lean on, rely on, and remain confident in God to work in my challenge, I saw how He fulfilled His promises. Each challenge I faced followed the same pattern. See if your experiences follow this cycle. Start at 'face a challenge' and go clockwise.

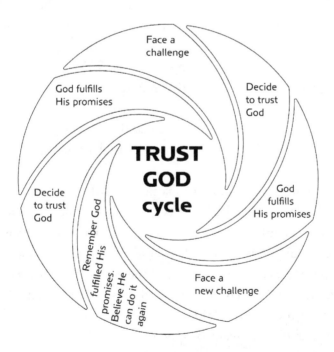

Maybe this Trust God cycle is a bit abstract. I'll walk you through it with a personal example. A new challenge (4th sliver of the cycle)

rudely intersected my path in the early hours of Thanksgiving day in 2021. Stabbing pains in my right lower abdomen were severe enough to warrant an Emergency Room visit. Despite believing my appendix was responsible, a CT scan revealed my colon had flipped upside down and was obstructed. The term for this rare medical occurrence is cecal volvulus.

Emergency surgery was scheduled. While I waited to be taken to the operating room, the unknowns of this new challenge filled my mind. How much of my colon will be removed? Will I have a colostomy bag for the rest of my life? How will my health be impacted? Will I have to change my diet? And a few other TMI questions I won't share!

Those questions invited anxiety and fear into the challenge. Instead of accepting their invitation, I thought about the weeks leading up to my brain surgery in 2016. Numerous fear and anxiety-inducing questions filled my mind back then. I remembered a dozen different messages of 'God's got this' invited me to trust Him. I accepted that invitation back then and truly experienced the peace that passes understanding (Philippians 4:7).

Memories of God fulfilling His promises during my surgery and recovery flooded my mind. My confidence and faith grew exponentially during those months. Despite the scariness of this new challenge, I knew God could do it again (5th sliver of the cycle). I decided to trust Him in this new challenge (6th sliver of the cycle). And once again, God protected me and cared for me during and since that challenge, strengthening my trust and faith in Him even more.

A regular dental cleaning appointment followed several months after my colon surgery. My dentist, Dr. Cole, came in to check my teeth. He read the notes the dental hygienist made about my colon surgery. "Wow! How are you doing?" he asked. "The doctor took half my colon, but I'm doing great!" I replied. I'll never forget his response. He said, "Oh! So now you're a semicolon!" Indeed, I am!

Describe how remembering God fulfilling His promises in your last challenge helps you move forward into believing He could do it again in your new challenge.

FOUND TRUE NOURISHMENT

As you read Christine's story, jot a note in the margins about which part of the trust cycle she's in.

When I interviewed Christine ^A in 2017, the focus of our discussion was her thirty-year challenge with obesity. Because she was disciplined with various weight loss plans during college through her late forties, she lost some weight. However, when all that weight returned, Christine knew a deeper-rooted problem existed.

A planned hike with her husband, Rob, on their twenty-fifth anniversary trip became Christine's turning point. Each mile of the flat path was plenty challenging. Rob then suggested they continue their hike on a path that was mostly uphill. Christine knew she wouldn't make it, so she encouraged him to continue the hike without her. She found a tree stump, sat down, and began reflecting on her life. Exasperated about her decades of unhealthiness, she cried out to God, "You have to help me."

He answered. In addition to discovering tools to reverse her chronic health issues, God impressed on Christine that studying His Word was an integral part of regaining her health. Remember learning Nelson DeMille's wisdom that "some pilgrims have better road maps" in mile 04 of *Challenges Won't Stop Me?* God showed her a better road map. Instead of satisfying her physical, emotional, and spiritual needs with food, Christine found true nourishment every time she studied God's Word.

Connecting with God and studying 'the better map' strengthened her faith and built her trust in God. Throughout her weight loss journey, Christine prioritized her daily morning 'Bible & Beans' time. While drinking her coffee and studying her Bible, she connected with God. As a result, her trust deepened. Christine saw evidence that God was with her,  equipping and empowering her to fight to overcome her food addiction. God's promises proved trustworthy time and time again. Over the course of a year and a half, Christine lost more than one hundred pounds.

HE COULD DO IT AGAIN

Just on the heels of reaching her goal weight in 2017, Christine's son, Kyle, was involved in a catastrophic car accident that led to numerous unexpected challenges. Upon arriving at the hospital, Christine and Rob learned Kyle had been unconscious for an undetermined amount of time. While they were grateful Kyle didn't need surgery and hadn't lost any limbs, they were surprised when he was discharged later that day.

Not long after the accident, Christine and Rob noticed how easily Kyle became agitated. They encouraged him to see a doctor, but he wasn't interested. When Kyle didn't feel comfortable completing the driving tasks associated with his job, he quit. Soon after, he sunk into a

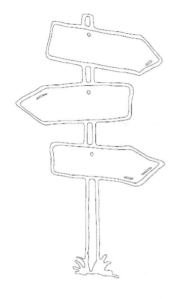

deep depression. Again, Christine and Rob begged Kyle to see a doctor.

Experiencing God's love, closeness, and healing during her weight-loss journey proved God was trustworthy. If He took care of her then, Christine believed He could do it again. All those mornings of learning how God responded to various Bible characters' challenges deepened her trust. If He responded to their challenges, Christine believed God would respond to Kyle's challenges. Declaring she trusted God gave Christine confidence to keep moving forward in faith. Trusting God would be a decision she would have to make again and again as Kyle continued to struggle.

Nearly two years later, Christine was at her wit's end with Kyle's behaviors, so she tried a different approach. "Kyle was not himself. We were living with a different person, so the best thing I could do was get myself some mental health therapy," she explained. "In God's divine intervention, I was assigned to a licensed mental health therapist who was also a neuropsychologist with experience in treating patients with brain injuries." There was no doubt that God was fighting for her and for Kyle.

During her first few therapy sessions, Christine shared her frustrations about the changes in her son. Several weeks later at a family session with Christine, Kyle, and Rob, a discussion about the behaviors Kyle began exhibiting after his car accident allowed the therapist to put all the pieces together. She said, "Kyle probably has a traumatic brain injury." While those words were hard to hear, Kyle was relieved to know he wasn't crazy. Filled with hope, Kyle agreed to receive treatment.

Just as one challenge seemed to be resolving, a larger, more frustrating challenge loomed just around the corner. "Because Kyle had been in a car accident, our insurance was involved. They didn't want to pay for his treatments and therapies. They fought us every step of the way," Christine explained. Each time she felt anger rising, she read Psalm 37.

Please go to biblegateway.com. Look up Psalm 37, verses 3 and 5 in the Amplified Bible, Classic Edition (AMPC). Write each below.

Psalm 37:3

Psalm 37:5

Unfortunately, suing the insurance company became necessary. The large insurance company believed they shouldn't have to pay for Kyle's treatments, medications, and therapies because he didn't receive a diagnosis until two years after the accident. Christine's carabiner kept her safely connected to God when the court battle felt out of control.

Remembering God fought for her during her weight loss journey proved God could be trusted again. Her 'challenges won't stop me' mindset carried her through, even when the court battle didn't end the way she and Rob expected. At the end of her second story interview in 2023, Christine shared this powerful wisdom: "My job is to trust God. God's job is the outcome."

Highlight the previous two sentences. Pause for a moment and think about the wisdom Christine shared. Describe why you agree or disagree with her.

TURNED TO INVESTIGATE

Like Christine, Tiffany[B] made studying God's Word and spending time in prayer a priority. Leading worship at church and inviting others to focus on God carried over into her personal life.

Notice Tiffany using her essential gear? Not only did she consistently use her map, multi-purpose tool, and binoculars, she spent time in God's tent, trusted Jesus to light her path, and recorded her journey in her travel log. No, Tiffany isn't a goody-two-shoes. She discovered early on in her life that her essential gear connected her to God, which strengthened her faith and built her trust in God.

Like Kyle, a catastrophic challenge intersected Tiffany's path in 2017 while she and her husband were on an anniversary cruise in the Bahamas. A day excursion that included snorkeling seemed like a great adventure. However, a rough boat ride out to the snorkeling site made Tiffany's husband, JJ, seasick. Wanting to enjoy the day, he jumped in the water. Twenty minutes of snorkeling made him feel worse, so he returned to the boat. Tiffany continued to snorkel among the colorful fish.

When Tiffany felt something bump her right arm, she turned to investigate. A shark stared back at her. Her right arm up to her elbow was in its mouth. Fear invaded her mind, but the Lord began infusing her with the strength to fight. She remembers thinking, *No! You will not take my life! I will not die here!* She yanked her arm, trying to free it. The shark wasn't interested in letting her go. She and the shark thrashed about until it finally backed off with her arm in its mouth.

Tiffany looked at what remained of her arm. Her blood was turning the water red. She surfaced the water and cried out, "Help! Help me, Jesus!" No one from the boat heard her thrashing nor did they hear her call for help. She began swimming toward the boat, continuing to call out for help. When this crisis intersected Tiffany's life, God's promises being fulfilled during previous challenges made it easy for her to trust God in this challenge. Tiffany knew her strong connection to God meant He wouldn't let her become unattached.

When her husband finally heard her cry for help, he jumped into the water and swam to her. With the captain's help, JJ lifted her into the boat. Tiffany needed immediate medical attention. Surprisingly, the boat lacked a medical kit *and* a radio to call for help. Would she trust God? Tiffany pointed to the fluffy towel she'd brought from the cruise ship. She said, "Make a tourniquet, JJ." After JJ secured the towel tightly around her wounded arm, the captain started the boat. Tiffany and JJ cried out to God while the boat headed toward Paradise Island.

DREW ME OUT OF DEEP WATERS

Even from a distance, tourists could be seen on the beach. "We need medical attention! Where's the hospital?" JJ shouted as the boat neared the shore. Several tourists shouted back, "This is a tourist island. There aren't any hospitals here. Go back to the main island."

Tiffany remembered the boat ride took twenty minutes to get from the port to where they snorkeled. Panic flooded her mind. Again, she chose to trust God. The boat finally arrived at the hospital. Doctors quickly assessed her wounds and sent her to the operating room. Several hours later, she gazed at the bandages covering her amputated arm.

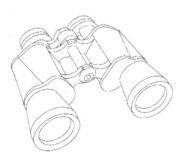

Tiffany read Psalm 18:16-17 several times over the years, but after surviving a shark attack, those verses took on a much deeper meaning. The passage reads, "He reached down from on high and took hold of me; he drew me out of deep waters. He rescued me from my powerful enemy, from my foes, who were too strong for me."

During her recovery, Tiffany lifted her binoculars to praise God for:

- Stopping the shark from pulling her deeper underwater when she was thrashing, which is in a shark's nature.
- Surrounding her with a tangible peace.
- Preventing other sharks from joining her attacker when her blood flooded the water.
- Allowing the makeshift towel tourniquet to stop the blood flow until she could get medical attention.
- Keeping her alive during the lengthy boat ride to the hospital.
- Not needing any blood transfusions. Her doctors said the absence of a medical kit and the lengthy amount of time it took to get help should have caused her to bleed out.

After hearing Tiffany describe these outcomes, it is abundantly clear God intervened multiple times to save her life. As she said, "He used every avenue beyond what I can understand to provide supernaturally."

Medical bills began filling their mailbox. The amount of money due was far beyond anything they could pay. Tiffany and JJ prayed, putting their trust in God. An answer to their prayers came when their insurance company wrote off most of her medical bills. Additionally, an anonymous donor covered the remainder. Once again God provided supernaturally. JJ and Tiffany praised God for covering her medical bills, which amounted to hundreds of thousands of dollars.

Should Tiffany need a reminder of God's faithfulness, she just has to look at the words grafted into her prosthetic arm: "God rescued me." During her interview, Tiffany shared, "I'm not even supposed to be here. God rescued me. And He saw in me something to give me this second chance. He rescued me for a purpose." Indeed, He did!

Since then, Tiffany's written two devotionals about maintaining endurance during challenging times. With student and adult audiences, she shares her story of God rescuing her. Tiffany's ministry is appropriately named 'Be an Overcomer.' She and JJ continue to take anniversary trips to invest in their marriage, including ones to the beach.

CHOOSING TO STAY CONNECTED TO GOD

Whew! Your carabiner truly is a safety-critical system *you can trust.* Attach one to a loop on your back-pack. Remember all God's done in your previous challenges when this next mile stretches you. If He did it then, He can do it again. Keep moving forward, believing whatever challenge intersects your path, it won't stop you!

Getting knocked down in life is a given. Getting up and moving forward is a choice! 3

—author and motivational speaker, Zig Ziglar

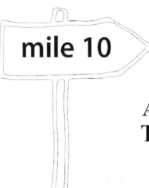

mile 10

Are You Growing and Thriving Despite Your Challenges?

Life moves forward. The old leaves wither, die and fall away,

and the new growth extends forward into the light.1

—Bryant McGill, author

See that clearing ahead? It's a protected space. Just for you. Drop your backpack by the oak tree. Look up. Take in the beauty all around you. Tune your ears to the silence. Breathe deeply. God is here with you.

Perhaps you're rolling your eyes. You don't have time to enjoy the silence. Not even a second to spare. Too many activities to juggle, an abundance of tasks on your to-do list, and all your family's laundry doesn't wash, dry, and fold itself. I won't argue that those activities may need your attention, but I will try to impress upon you that you *desperately* need this time.

Notice the oak tree is not part of a cluster of trees. This oak tree stands alone. Each of us grow and thrive in unique ways, so spending a bit of time alone will give you space to focus on *your* growth. And you won't be distracted by anyone else's growth.

The solitary oak tree in the clearing represents growth. Bear with me as connecting expected encounters to visual images does have its limitations. A tree is entirely too large to fit in your backpack, so acorns and leaves will be the visual image for growth.

A THOUSAND FORESTS

One winter day when Martin was ten years old, his dad took him to their pasture to plant acorns. While they dug holes, his dad said, "My favorite poet, Ralph Waldo Emerson, once said, 'The creation of a thousand forests is in one acorn.' [2] Sometime in the future, son, you'll return to this pasture and see a forest of mighty oaks."

Twenty years later, after his dad's funeral, Martin returned to that pasture. "I see the forest of mighty oaks you predicted, Dad. Tomorrow, I plan to pass on all you taught me about trees to Theo." Martin lingered for a while, recalling the times he'd spent sitting under the sturdy branches of those mighty oaks with his dad.

As you read the following story, highlight references to growth. Underline any challenges that could negatively impact growth.

The next day, Martin watched as Theo dug a hole and buried an acorn. He crouched down next to his twelve-year-old son. "An acorn is the beginning of what will become a mighty oak tree. In twenty years, the mature oak tree will begin producing acorns. Maybe a Danger Ahead sign should be nearby to warn those acorns of the challenges they'll experience when they fall from the tree," Martin said.

"I don't get it, Dad. Why a Danger Ahead sign?" Theo asked. Martin laughed. "To warn those acorns of the dangers awaiting them! Warning them to watch out for the humans who will narrowly avoid stepping on them. And for the blue jays who swoop down to the ground, looking for a snack. Making it through those challenges is no small feat," Martin said. "Not to mention the heavy rainfalls that threaten to flush those acorns down the sewers. I remember your grandfather saying, 'If an acorn can survive all those obstacles, it's meant to thrive!'"

"The acorns that land near favorable soil conditions, adequate moisture, and medium sunlight will begin germinating. Other acorns will be carried to a squirrel's dark burrow. The warm temperatures in that dark environment cause the seed inside the acorn to burst through the shell. Its taproots begin growing down into the dirt," Martin shared.

Despite the growth that occurs in a burrow, many dislike this dark, lonely place. It might feel like a setback, but it's actually a setup. A setup to grow vigorously. Describe your growth during a time you felt buried.

SPREAD AND GROW STRONGER

After eating a snack, Martin and Theo returned to the task of planting acorns. Martin pointed to several scrawny trees and then to a row of mature trees. "Theo, what do you think caused the difference in those trees?"

"Mr. Wilson told us what we see above the dirt is directly related to everything that happens or doesn't happen in the dirt," Theo replied. Thick pollen in the air caused Theo to sneeze and then he continued, "Plants and trees have two kinds of roots." Theo stretched his arms wide and then up high while explaining, "One type of root spreads horizontally, and the other spreads vertically. The horizontal roots are the anchor. The vertical roots soak up rainwater and nutrients from the soil, which are food for the tree."

"Nice job! Can you describe the difference between the roots of those scrawny trees and the roots of those mature trees?" Martin asked. "Well, Dad, when a tree is well taken care of, the horizontal roots spread and grow stronger, and the vertical roots grow deeper. Mr.

Wilson told us nutrient-rich soil, the right amount of sunlight, and plenty of rainwater aren't just recommendations. They are necessities."

"Those scrawny trees over there probably didn't get enough of one of more of those necessities, so their roots didn't grow strong and deep. And those mature trees got nice tans while slurping down tall glasses of refreshing water and eating bacon double cheeseburgers!" Theo's laughter was contagious. "Great explanation, Theo! I wasn't expecting your unique spin," Martin replied.

Martin dropped an acorn in the hole he'd dug. "Grandad and I walked this pasture when I was your age. He showed me the trees he planted with his dad that had survived hail or forceful winds. Some looked like those scrawny trees because they endured several years of drought. Unfortunately, my favorite oak was struck by lightning and died."

"Other things like digging or parking heavy construction machinery too close to the base of a tree can damage its roots. Gypsy moths and tent caterpillars eat the bark of an infected or weakened tree, causing it to die. Fungal diseases are vicious because they spread infection throughout weakened trees. Just like your grandad said, when you know all the challenges a tree faces, it is a big deal to see a healthy one."

"Nice job, Dad. Mr. Wilson would give you an A+. Can we get lunch? I'm starving. I'm thinking bacon double cheeseburgers." Martin grabbed their shovels and started walking toward the truck. "You bet, son."

THE STRENGTH OF YOUR ROOT SYSTEM

Theo obviously learned a great deal about the root system of a tree from his teacher, Mr. Wilson, who said, "What we see above the dirt is directly related to everything that happens or doesn't happen in the dirt." A tree's root system is indeed critical to its growth. It's critical to your growth too. What you see 'above dirt' or happening in your life is directly related to the strength and depth of 'everything happening in the dirt,' or in your root system.

Take a moment to assess your root system. Is it well-nourished? Are your roots growing deeper and stronger? Will your root system be strong enough to anchor you when tough challenges intersect your path in the future?

Your root system is directly connected to your spiritual life. Your relationship with God directly impacts whether your roots are shallow or deep. Weak or strong. A tree's roots grow wide, strong, and deep by receiving nutrient-rich soil, the right amount of sunlight, and plenty of rainwater. We see in God's Word that we need those same ingredients to grow spiritual roots that are wide, strong, and deep:

"Still other seed fell on *good soil*. It came up and yielded a crop, a hundred times more than was sown" (Luke 8:8).

"The path of the righteous is like *the morning sun*, shining ever brighter till the full light of day" (Proverbs 4:18).

"Blessed is the one who ... is like a tree planted by *streams of water*, which yields fruit in season and whose leaf does not wither—whatever they do prospers" (Psalm 1:1, 3).

Good soil, morning sun, and streams of water yield a healthy root system, which spreads wide, is strong, and grows deep. A tree's roots grow in dirt. Where do your roots grow? The apostle Paul explained, "So then, just as you received Christ Jesus as Lord, continue to live your lives in him, *rooted* and built up in him, strengthened in the faith as you were taught, and overflowing with thankfulness" (Colossians 2:6-7).

Based on these verses, in whom do your roots grow?

Besides good soil, the morning sun, and streams of water, what else is identified in these verses as necessities for growing a healthy root system?

Are you *rooted* in Him? If so, describe what being *rooted* in Him looks like.

A HEALTHY ROOT SYSTEM

What happens when lightning strikes and slices through your heart? When hurricane winds gust so forcefully you are certain you will break? When enemies attack and spread infectious lies about you?

When quarter-sized hail repeatedly strikes your health? These challenges could stop you from growing. Will they? Not if your root system has spread wide, is strong, and is growing deep.

Your root system is activated when challenges like these intersect your life. How does your root system respond when lightning slices through your heart? Deep roots support you by nourishing you with God's unfailing 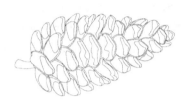 love. How about when hurricane force winds ravage your life? Strong roots anchor you, allowing you to adapt, to be flexible. Bending you but not breaking you. How does your root system respond when enemies spread infectious lies about you? Those deep roots uphold you in your true identity. You are God's chosen. You stand tall and confident.

How does your root system respond when hail repeatedly pounds your health? Those deep and strong roots shield you while you persevere until the hailstorm passes. A healthy root system doesn't ignore you or wish you the best when challenges intersect your life. Quite the opposite. A healthy root system supports you, anchors you, upholds you, and shields you.

Please highlight the last sentence in the previous paragraph.

Describe a time when your root system supported, anchored, upheld, and/or shielded you.

FRUITFUL GROWTH

Martin and Theo didn't discuss pruning as an integral part of maintaining a tree healthy, but we would be remiss to skip it. *Merriam-Webster* defines *prune* as "to reduce especially by eliminating superfluous matter; to cut off or cut back parts for better shape or more fruitful growth."

These definitions for prune contain painful words. It's hard to reconcile how reducing, eliminating, cutting off, and cutting back could possibly lead to healthy growth. But, what's dead, dying, infected, diseased, or hindering your growth is taking up valuable space. Pruning a tree opens space for new growth. Left to ourselves, we might rationalize why the dead, dying, or infected habits, relationships, or activities should be left alone. You know you should take out the pruning shears, but _____

_____ .

Below, list habits, relationships, or activities that are dead, dying, infected, or hindering your growth. Spend time reflecting to decide if it's time to pull out the pruning shears. If it is, beside each one, write whether you plan to 'reduce/ cut back' or 'eliminate/ cut off.'

ELIMINATE OUR SELF-RELIANCE

Pruning is a harsh and painful process. Resist being pruned and those dead, dying, infected, and hindering habits, relationships, and activities will overtake and block any space needed for your growth. Embrace the pruning process and that newly opened space will overflow with healthy and fruitful growth!

Pruning isn't limited to the dead, dying, and infected parts of our lives. Jesus addressed another reason for pruning in John 15:1-8. See if you spot it.

"I am the true vine, and my Father is the gardener. He cuts off every branch in me that bears no fruit, while every branch that does bear fruit he prunes so that it will be even more fruitful. You are already clean because of the word I have spoken to you. Remain in me, as I also remain in you. No branch can bear fruit by itself; it must remain in the vine. Neither can you bear fruit unless you remain in me. 'I am the vine; you are the branches. If you remain in me and I in you, you will bear much fruit; apart from me you can do nothing. If you do not remain in me, you are like a branch that is thrown away and withers; such branches are picked up, thrown into the fire and burned. If you remain in me and my words remain in you, ask whatever you wish, and it will be done for you. This is to my Father's glory, that you bear much fruit, showing yourselves to be my disciples.'"

Pruning dead, dying, or infected habits, relationships, or activities which are preventing us from growing makes sense. But being pruned when we are bearing fruit? Why then? Sometimes we are growing by trusting and relying on our skills, abilities, and connections instead of trusting and relying on God for our growth. His pruning shears eliminate our self-reliance.

Did you notice John 15 describes how abiding, or remaining in God, leads to healthy growth and bearing much fruit? When you attach your carabiner to God, you are abiding in Him. Trusting God for your growth by leaning on, relying on, and being confident in Him will lead to the fruitful growth He intends for you. Allow Him to prune you, and you will become even more fruitful!

Describe a time when you were bearing fruit and were pruned. How did you become even more fruitful?

Reread John 15:1-8 with your carabiner in mind. Highlight every instance of the word *remain*. Write the words *stay connected* above it.

When you exchanged *remain* with *stay connected*, what new insights did you gain?

GROW VIGOROUSLY

We like the idea of being healthy and fruitful, but growth is hard, frustrating, and slow work. *Merriam-Webster* defines *grow* as "to spring up and develop to maturity; to be able to grow in some place or situation; to increase; to expand; to have an increasing influence; to promote the development of."

While these definitions define *growth* well, Nobel prize winner Frances Arnold offered two additional definitions for *growth*. See if you spot them. She said, "To survive and even thrive in a changing world, nature offers another great lesson: the survivors are those who at the least adapt to change, or even better learn to benefit from change and grow intellectually and personally." [3]

Did you spot the phrases *adapt to change* and *learn to benefit from change*? Please highlight those phrases in Arnold's quote.

American inventor, Benjamin Franklin, once said, "In this world, nothing can be said to be certain except death and taxes." [4] I would argue that in this world change is certain. Change is as certain as hummingbirds migrating south for the winter.

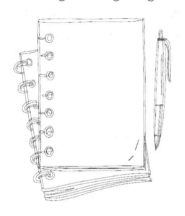

Adapting—fitting for a new use—to change, however, is a choice. You don't have to adapt. You can choose to tightly grasp your former ways, or you can choose to adapt and discover new ways. Adapting to change is not passive. You must actively engage your problem-solving skills, flexibility, and perseverance.

Your travel log—an essential piece of gear from mile 08 in *Challenges Won't Stop Me*—offers the space to record the changes invoked by your challenges or circumstances. Recording your journey allows you to visually see the ways you adapted to change during your challenge. And how you grew. With this perspective, you are able to see the lessons or the benefits of your challenges.

Let's look at the first part of Arnold's quote again. She said, "To survive and even thrive." You may remember that the word *thriving* is in the subtitle for both *Challenges Won't Stop Me* and *Keep Moving Forward*. We looked at the definition of *thrive* in mile 00 of *Challenges Won't Stop Me*. Let's look at it again. *Thrive* means "to grow vigorously; to flourish; to prosper; to progress toward or realize a goal despite or because of circumstances."

Highlight *to grow vigorously, to flourish,* **and** *despite or because of circumstance.*

Each of us grow in varying degrees when facing a challenge. But not all will thrive. Why not? Thriving is more than growing. It is the result of challenges or circumstances threatening to defeat and destroy you, but you didn't cooperate. Some people give in or give up when challenges threaten to defeat or stop them. You didn't. Instead, you adapted. You persevered. You fought to overcome. You noticed all the ways those challenges benefited you. Because of these choices, you grew vigorously and flourished despite the challenges. That, my friend, is thriving!

Please highlight "You grew vigorously and flourished despite the challenges." Double underline *despite the challenges*.

SLAM INTO SILENCE

As we proceed, you might think we took a sharp turn into a foreign land. No need to worry. I'm following the map. I'm certain you agree that fighting to overcome life's tough challenges is exhausting. Add in the growth that occurs, and it's surprising we're still standing.

Perhaps you need a 'time out.' Remember being sent to 'time out' for misbehaving when you were a kid? I do! You haven't misbehaved, but you do need space and time to process everything your mind, emotions, body, and spirit have endured during your challenges. Solitude and silence offer that space.

You may feel awkward or uncomfortable being alone in this silent space. Everything in you might rebel. Within a few minutes, you might even experience boredom. Sadly, most of us don't know what to do when the demands cease. And our noisy lives slam into silence. This silence may roar louder than all the noises in your life combined.

For some, silence is as painful as a yearly mammogram. Like mammograms, those people know they should make time for solitude, but they don't look forward to it and are glad when it's over. Others believe silence is like wrapping up in a blanket right out of the dryer. Hours alone, basking in the comfort of beautiful silence, is sheer bliss to them.

If you practice silence and solitude, describe the positive outcomes you've experienced.

If you haven't practiced silence and solitude, what hesitations do you have?

A SECURE PLACE IN A NOISY WORLD

King David knew the immeasurable benefits of intentionally separating himself from the noise of the world. In Psalm 27:4-5, David shared the benefits he received when he spent time in silence and solitude: "I'm asking GOD for one thing, only one thing: to live with him in his house my whole life long. I'll contemplate his beauty; I'll study at his feet. That's the only quiet, secure place in a noisy world, the perfect getaway, far from the buzz of traffic" (MSG).

Describe why David would want to spend time with God in the only quiet, secure place in a noisy world.

God is in this quiet, secure place. He is eager to speak to you. To guide you. To teach you. To lavish you in His unfailing love. To point out all the ways you're growing. Ah, but there is one expectation for hearing His voice. You *must* listen.

You might find it surprising that during a conversation the average person listens about twenty-five percent of the time. What happens the other seventy-five percent of the time? Research says we are forming our response. As such, we are eager to share our opinions, our interpretation of the situation, our wishes, our ideas, and our advice. Instead of listening.

When we aren't listening, we often miss details the other person is communicating. Or *trying* to communicate. Really listening is challenging when you are chatting with a visible person. Multiply that challenge by a million when you are listening for an invisible God to speak.

Whenever you seek Him in silence and solitude, imagine God's gaze focused solely on you. No other conversations are pulling His attention away from you. He isn't wishing you'd just hurry up, so He can get to his next task or appointment. The smile stretched across God's face communicates His adoration and love for you. There's a twinkle in His eye because you've chosen to seek Him and spend time with Him.

Allow these descriptions of God's 'listening' posture to encourage you. Don't forget to tune your ear to Him and listen for His voice. He's eager to communicate with you.

Please highlight *His attention is directed solely at you. He's not in a hurry. A smile is stretched across His face. And there is a twinkle in His eye.*

Describe how these descriptions of God's 'listening' posture toward you impacts you.

CONNECT WITH HIM

Ever notice how we often don't see our growth? Or realize we're thriving? Growth is sometimes easier to see in others. I believe it's easy to spot in Lisa and Zoe's stories.

Overcomers Lisa and Zoe faced difficult challenges. As you read each overcomer's story, look for and mark her mindset about the challenges, how she consistently used her essential gear, the growth she experienced, and how silence and solitude were an integral part of her journey.

Being fully committed to her marriage made it difficult for Lisa ^C to understand her husband's lack of emotional attachment. A few years into their marriage, she began to wonder if she was the cause. She wondered, *Am I fulfilling the vows I made to him? Do I encourage him and express my love for him in ways that he feels it? Am I supporting his work and engaging in activities that interest him?* She knew she wasn't a perfect wife, but Lisa was devoted to him and truly loved him.

Over the next few years of their marriage, her husband's emotional withdrawal intensified. His profound mood swings sent Lisa spinning as she didn't understand how to connect with him. Having children didn't bring them closer. In fact, the normal stressors of having a family escalated his disturbing behaviors. "He stopped responding to the needs of our family. He no longer engaged on an emotional level with me or our children. I noticed he was inappropriately flirting with other women and had been our whole marriage," Lisa shared.

INFIDELITY AND ADDICTION

Two of Lisa's children found websites for soliciting prostitutes on their dad's computer. They confronted him, but he denied he had a problem. He manipulated his children into not telling Lisa about the websites on his computer. Almost a year later, another one of their children found links to massage parlors and requests to solicit prostitutes on his computer.

No longer willing to keep his secrets, Lisa's three children shared their disturbing findings with her. An intervention with a counselor followed. Lisa's husband minimized the concrete evidence of his infidelity and addiction. Several men of strong faith spent time praying with him and trying to hold him accountable. Her husband met with multiple counselors, but his actions never matched his commitment to change.

Having built a solid foundation of prayer and Bible study in college, Lisa leaned hard on her faith. "God carried me through. He comforted me daily," she explained. Lisa sought silence and solitude so she could pour out her heart in prayer. She waited for God's direction during the four and a half years of fighting for their marriage. She believed Exodus 14:14, which says, "The LORD will fight for you; you need only to be still."

Despite forgiving him and standing by him, her husband's heart was hardened. He chose to continue his life of deception. Eventually, their marriage ended in divorce. While divorce was a challenge she never wanted, Lisa took time to process it and grow from it. In the years since their divorce, teaching ladies' Bible studies, leading trips to the Holy Land, and taking mission trips fill Lisa's heart with joy.

THE ENEMY'S CLAWS

Zoe ^D (a pseudonym to protect her identity) endured horrific trauma as a child. When she was just six years old, her father burned down the house with Zoe and her sister in it. Her best friend's house wasn't any safer. Her best friend's stepfather sexually abused her and groomed her to participate in a satanic cult.

Zoe was then forced into a satanic marriage at age ten, followed by a pregnancy, and an abortion at age twelve. "Whatever was inside of me died. It left me feeling I would never be accepted. I would never be whole," Zoe shared.

For years, Zoe struggled. How does a young adult process the unexplainable? Her body reeled from the physical trauma. Her mind repeated the lies over and over, embedding their evil deep in her soul. Her emotions were stretched as thin as rice paper.

Her response? Cutting, bulimia, alcohol, and suicide attempts. Flashbacks of all the trauma and pain she endured crippled her. The enemy's claws burrowed deep into her soul, slowly and methodically ripping her apart.

In her early twenties, Zoe began attending church with a friend. Everything she experienced and learned about God at that church was in direct opposition to all she'd been exposed to and forced to accept about herself. After several months of hearing God's Word, she asked for a meeting with the pastor. Zoe found the courage to confess the horrors that had been perpetrated against her.

All the lies spilled out, opening the fortified dam she had constructed long ago. In the conversation with the pastor, Zoe explained, "If there's a chance God would forgive me and cleanse me, that's the only hope I have left." The pastor assured Zoe that God would forgive her *and* cleanse her. She accepted Christ that day, declaring, "For the first time, I knew what hope was. I was given a new life."

AN INTEGRAL PART OF HER WALK WITH CHRIST

In the years since accepting Christ, the enemy has not backed off Zoe. He often waits until she feels distant from God to remind her of the pain others inflicted upon her and the atrocities done to her. Where does Zoe go when she's under attack? She goes where David went: "The only quiet, secure place in a noisy world."

Zoe's quiet and secure place is the monastery. After a weekend retreat at the monastery, I asked her to explain how spending time there impacted her. Her face lit up. Words tumbled out of her mouth faster than my ears could process. "It's silent. It's peaceful. I know God is everywhere, but He's really there," she said. "I can practice solitude and listen for God's voice. I hear His voice there. All the distractions are taken away."

Hearing God's voice? For real? After thirty minutes of non-stop descriptions about how God's Presence was palpable and all He revealed to her there, I called the next day and scheduled a silent weekend retreat at the monastery. That was years ago. Zoe has returned to the monastery numerous times since then. And so have I.

Zoe and I met for coffee after my second silent retreat at the monastery. We discussed how integral solitude and silence are to our lives. She described silence and solitude as "an intentional separation from the world in order to create space for me and my Creator. It facilitates deep vulnerability with the Lord. Isolation, the opposite of solitude, closes my heart to pain and healing, while solitude offers up my hurting heart to the one who can make it new. Solitude breathes life into my soul, so that when I reconnect  with the world, I do so with a heart that has experienced healing and remaking."

Zoe's currently pursuing a seminary degree. When she graduates, she's eager to return to the mission field. Spending time with her nieces fills her with joy.

Reread Zoe's quote in the paragraph next to the cup of coffee. Sit with her words for a moment. Are you intentionally creating space for God?

What would it look like and feel like to experience Him breathing 'life into your soul'?

WITHDREW TO LONELY PLACES

Jesus spent time in silence and solitude. He "withdrew by boat privately to a solitary place" (Matthew 14:13), "went up on a mountainside by himself to pray" (Matthew 14:23), "went off to a solitary place where he prayed" (Mark 1:35), "withdrew to lonely places and prayed" (Luke 5:16), and "prayed in private" (Luke 9:18).

In each of these verses, Jesus intentionally separated himself from the disciples or from the crowds to pray and commune with God. In John 7:10, Jesus walked to the Festival of Tabernacles "not publicly, but in secret." Bible scholars believe Jesus walked the ninety miles from Galilee to Jerusalem in solitude. That's a lot of silence! When Jesus spent time in those solitary, lonely, private, and secret places, I believe His Father's voice encouraged Him to keep moving forward in His purpose.

Are you willing to take a moment right now to follow Jesus' example?

Silence the noise around you. I'll do the same, so we can hear God's voice. I'd invite you to join me, but well ... that defeats the purpose of silence and solitude. Perhaps you could sit under the tree by the fence. I'll sit under the tree on the other side of the stream.

Meet back in a couple of hours? I can't wait to hear how God encouraged you by pointing out how vigorously you're growing despite all the challenges you've faced. Grab a few acorns and leaves. Throw them in your backpack. Let's journey on!

> Their strength is their secret. They send ferocious roots beneath the ground … Four who grew despite concrete. Four who reach and do not forget to reach.4
>
> —Author Sandra Cisneros

mile 11

Are Your Challenges Consuming You or Refining You?

And out of the deepest waters and the hottest fires have come the deepest things I know about God.1

—Elisabeth Elliot, missionary and author

A s we continue our journey, I must warn you. The refining fires ahead will be the most painful of all the expected encounters. No one enjoys the refining process, but this invaluable process is necessary to develop God's character in you. A stronger, more resilient, and more fruitful you.

Please highlight *develop God's character in you.*

List one or more of God's character traits you desire to be developed in you.

Reread the opening quote by Elisabeth Elliott. Describe one or more deep things you know about God only because you have endured a refining fire.

The refining fires allow God to develop—to promote the growth of —His character in you. The unrelenting heat will zap your strength. Your soul will be rubbed raw. And the blazing flames will reduce you to ashes. Don't be alarmed. God promises those ashes will be transformed into beauty.

Isaiah, through the LORD's anointing, described how Jesus will "bestow on them a crown of beauty instead of ashes, the oil of joy instead of mourning, and a garment of praise instead of despair. They will be called oaks of righteousness, a planting of the LORD for the display of his splendor" (Isaiah 61:1,3).

While these verses are most often quoted regarding a refining fire, did you also notice that those who are bestowed with beauty, joy, and praise are called oaks of righteousness? Your refining fires are growing you into an oak of righteousness!

The obvious visual image for this mile would be a fire, but putting a fire in our backpack is definitely not wise. So, a box of matches will represent refining fire.

SILVER THROUGH A REFINING FIRE

In the middle of Psalm 66, David described several of the ways God tested the Israelites, which included being refined by fire. Notice the outcome of those tests as you read verses 8-12: "Praise our God, all peoples, let the sound of his praise be heard; he has preserved our lives and kept our feet from slipping. For you, God, tested us; you refined us like silver. You brought us into prison and laid burdens on our backs. You let people ride over our heads; we went through fire and water, but you brought us to a place of abundance."

Write one or more of the phrases from Psalm 66:8-12 that accurately describe a recent challenge or your current challenge.

Chances are you can easily recall experiencing one or more of the phrases described in Psalm 66. For this mile, we will focus on the phrase 'you refined us like silver.' *Merriam-Webster* defines *refine* as "to free something from impurities, or unwanted material; to free from moral imperfection; to improve by pruning or polishing; to free from what is coarse, uncouth, or vulgar; and to become pure and perfected."

In the definition above, please highlight *to free (3x)*, *to improve*, and *to become*.

To *free from, to improve,* and *to become* are the beautiful outcomes of the refining process. Think about a refining fire you experienced and its intended outcomes of freeing you, improving you, and helping you to become pure and perfected.

Describe how your ashes were replaced with a 'crown of beauty' (Isaiah 61:3).

PRECIOUS AND OF GREAT VALUE

Given the outward appearance of silver when it's first mined would lead some to believe it's not worthy or not valuable. A silversmith would quickly correct that false assumption. Instead, he would explain the 'who' (you) or 'what'(silver/gold) that is put through a refining fire is precious, of great value, and highly esteemed.

Because this concept is so important, please double underline *precious, of great value,* and *highly esteemed* in the previous sentence.

Satan will try to convince you the weeks, months, or years of your refining fire will consume you, or "to do away with completely; to destroy; to devour; to waste away." Don't listen to or believe his lies. He is the one who desires to consume you. Please allow me to remind you that God's purpose for your refining fires is to develop—or to promote the growth of—His character in you. Therefore, you *will not* be done away with completely. Nor will you be destroyed or devoured. And you won't waste away. Quite the opposite.

God is freeing you from impurities, freeing you from moral imperfection, improving you by polishing you, and freeing you from what is coarse, uncouth, or vulgar in your life. You are becoming pure and perfected!

SEPARATE THE SILVER FROM IMPURITIES

As you read the process a silversmith uses when refining silver, highlight and number the eight steps in the process. Hint: the eighth step describes the exact time the silversmith removes the silver from the fire.

Silver extracted from the earth is a precious metal, but you'd never know it by its appearance. Silver in its natural state isn't silver in color, nor is it shiny. Impurities in natural silver cause it to be dull and mask its true beauty.

The first step of the process is to crush the silver several times. Then, it's pulverized to a fine powder. Flux, an agitator, is added to the powder to separate the silver from impurities. Next, this combination of metal and agitator is placed in a cauldron and held over a fire. Not just any location in the fire will do.

The cauldron must be held where the flame is the hottest. Because the silver is 'precious, of great value, and highly esteemed,' the silversmith never takes his eye off the fire. As impurities rise to the surface, the silversmith removes the cauldron from the fire and scrapes off the dross, which is the scum or unwanted material that forms on the surface of the silver. Then, he returns the cauldron to the fire, reheating the silver at a higher temperature. Additional dross rises to the surface and is scraped off.

Is it time to remove the silver from the fire? Maybe. The silversmith knows the silver is fully refined when he can see his image in the hot silver liquid. Only then does he remove it from the fire. His timing must be impeccable, for if the cauldron sits in the fire just one moment too long, the silver will be destroyed.

LOOKING FOR HIS IMAGE

Did you find all eight steps of the refining process? If you did, great job! If not, here they are: 1. Crushing you. 2. Pulverizing you to a fine powder. 3. Agitating you to separate the impurities from your heart and mind. 4. Holding you over the hottest flame for a specific amount of time. 5. Scraping off the dross. 6. Reheating you at an even higher temperature. 7. Scraping off more scum. 8. Waiting patiently until He sees His image when He looks at you.

In God's infinite wisdom, the purpose of His refining fires is for you to become more like Him. Only when His image emerges does God remove you from the fire. He won't wait too long as He has no intention of destroying you. You are *very precious and of great value* to God.

Let's seek to understand what God intended when your path led you to a refining fire. Think of that time. Describe what occurred at each step of the process.

1. Crushed

2. Pulverized to a fine powder

3. Agitators added

4. Held over the fire

5. Dross scraped away

6. Reheated with an even hotter fire

7. Additional dross scraped away

8. Removed when God saw His image in you

How long did your refining process last?

Describe how you looked more like God when you emerged from the refining fire.

PLACE OF ABUNDANCE

Verse 12 of Psalm 66 that we read at the beginning of this mile says, "but you brought us to a place of abundance." Finally? Yes, hallelujah! God brought the Israelites to a place of abundance. You might know it as the Promised Land or 'a land flowing with milk and honey.'

Commentaries describe this place of abundance with words like overflow, well-watered, and refreshment. This refreshing, overflowing, and abundant place is God's promise for you *after* you've made it through the refining fire. A bit of time may need to pass before you can see and appreciate your place of abundance.

You may not see your beauty, but others do. They see a difference in you. People are curious about this polished you. What they see is how you navigate life differently. How you confidently accept new and hard things. How you embody joy even when you are in pain. They see how wisdom shapes your words and actions. And how gratitude flows out of you. Your growth is unmistakable. Being in this place of abundance also positions you to impact the lives of those around you.

FOUR POWERFUL LETTERS

Multiple decades describe the length of Addlia's ^{E} refining fires. H-O-M-E—four powerful letters knit together. Many of us take the word home for granted. Not Addlia. Home has been a tough word all her life. Her parents' divorce divided her home. An abortion at sixteen left her reeling and feeling alone in her home. Another unplanned pregnancy left her without support and without a home. Needing help with her newborn son, Addlia moved into her best friend's home. But that refuge only lasted a year.

Addlia bought and ran a salon suite. Life seemed to be working in her favor. Unfortunately, serious health problems arose, causing a ripple effect. She was forced to close the salon, which meant her income was gone. In addition to her challenges, her aunt's home, whom she'd been living with, was being foreclosed. Now that home was gone, too.

After two months of living with a friend, Addlia was financially able to rent an apartment. But to keep this home, she juggled three jobs. Getting laid off several months later from all three jobs meant no income and no way to keep her apartment. Addlia took a job at a hotel, which laid her off a few months later.

SHAPING AND MOLDING HER

Addlia believed God developed His character traits in her by shaping and molding her in a refining fire. The refining process proved painful, but knowing God was with her gave her the strength to keep getting up, going to work, and maintaining a positive attitude. Finally, a job at a hair salon led to earning money again. Addlia also began working as a night auditor at a hotel and as an executive's personal assistant. These three jobs allowed her to save enough money to move into an apartment and buy a car.

Some of us have never thought twice about where we will sleep at night. Addlia, on the other hand, has fought and continues to fight hard to keep the four precious letters of H-O-M-E knit together. She's been in  God's refining fires for a long time, feeling the intense heat of homelessness, again and again. Every time God scraped away dross, Addlia felt the pain. Trusting Him wasn't ever in question, but she often pondered why He allowed her to face homelessness multiple times throughout her life.

Addlia explained in her interview, "God's refining fire burned away my need for validation from others. In those times of homelessness, I was alone and the only one left was God. I was backed so far into the corner I had no choice but to depend only on Him. And to look to God to validate me. He showed me who I am in Him. The refining fires burned away my self-neglect and self-condemnation. They burned away fear and every hindrance that was keeping me from being my truest self."

Addlia gives God all the credit for the doors of opportunity opening for her son to study nursing at his dream college. What is she up to as an empty nester? After saving enough money for a solid down payment, she is now a homeowner! It's been a long and difficult journey, but Addlia believes, "I'm loving the me that remains after the refining fires. It only makes me glow brighter!" You gotta love that kind of attitude!

Have your refining fires made you glow brighter? If so, describe your glow.

PROVEN GENUINENESS OF YOUR FAITH

The apostle Peter shared another outcome for refining fires. He said, "Pure gold put in the fire comes out of it proved pure; genuine faith put through this suffering comes out proved genuine. When Jesus wraps this all up, it's your faith, not your gold, that God will have on display as evidence of his victory" (1 Peter 1:6-7, MSG).

In these verses, Peter wants you to know your faith is what is being tested in the refining fire. Those fires test whether your faith has proved pure and genuine. So, what does 'proved pure' and 'genuine' have to do with faith? *Merriam-Webster* defines *proved* as "to establish the existence or validity of; to demonstrate as having a particular quality or worth."

Is your faith established? Is your faith of quality and worth? The refining fires will test your faith to find out. *Genuine* means "actually having the apparent qualities of character; actually produced by or proceeding from the author." The refining fires are testing if your character proceeds from God. Are your character traits God-like?

Please allow me to temporarily exchange the word 'gold' with the word 'faith' in the verses from 1 Peter 1:6. It would read, "Pure faith put in the fire comes out of it proved pure. Genuine faith put through this suffering comes out proved genuine." Whoa!

Describe how knowing refining fires are testing your faith impacts you.

What dross would need to be scraped off so that your faith would be proved pure and genuine?

EVIDENCE OF HIS VICTORY

Remember reading that the silversmith has a specific outcome in mind? So does God. Let's look at 1 Peter 1:7 again. It says, "It's your faith, not your gold, that God will have on display as evidence of his victory."

Why is God so focused on your faith? Having confidence in what we hope for and assurance in what we haven't seen is a big deal to God (Hebrews 11:1). Faith is very real, but we can't see it. Faith says you trust God with your earthly life, all while eagerly anticipating your heavenly life.

You didn't have to choose to lean on God when He could have healed your health struggles and didn't. But you did. You had faith that the months of pain and sleeplessness held purpose. You didn't have to choose to trust God when several relationships you valued suddenly disappeared, but you did. You had faith that He knew those relationships were hurting you and holding you back.

You didn't have to choose to rely on God when you were laid off from your job and your finances suffered greatly, but you did. You had faith that He would provide. You leaned on, relied on, and trusted God because you have confidence in and hope for the day that you will see His image face to face!

Describe your thoughts about "It's your faith that God will have on display as evidence of his victory."

GO THROUGH THE FIRE

"Get busy living instead of busy dying" has been Emmie's [F] motto for the last twenty-seven years. She's significantly surpassed her life expectancy, so each day is a gift to be treasured. Nine weeks into her pregnancy, her gynecologist recognized low hemoglobin levels. An iron deficiency or low B_{12} levels were suspected. No noticeable improvement occurred with the addition of iron tablets. Emmie began seeing a hematologist who suspected she had hemolytic anemia. Her pregnancy was elevated to a high-risk status.

During her interview, Emmie described a dream she had while she was in the hospital on bed rest. Her husband told her their baby was in the nursery, but they needed to talk about Emmie's health. She didn't know what Dennis meant, but the presence of God was profound in her dream. She explained, "God told me I'd go through the fire. He would be with me and give me peace."

At the thirty-three-week mark of her pregnancy, Emmie developed toxemia and preeclampsia. Whatever was causing her hemoglobin levels to be low was also causing her body to go into crisis mode. A spike in her blood pressure sent her into labor. Soon after her son was born, Emmie's kidneys and liver shut down. She began throwing blood clots. Her red blood cell counts plummeted.

Emmie met with the hematologist a few weeks after her son's birth. "When the results came back, I learned I tested positive for Paroxysmal Nocturnal Hemoglobinuria (PNH). My doctor shared that my rare bone marrow disorder wasn't hereditary but acquired. I was a level three with 90% of my blood cells affected. As scary as the diagnosis was, at least I knew what my disease was called," she shared.

HAS NOT DESTROYED HER

The refining fire God predicted in her dream came on with a vengeance and hotter than Emmie thought she could endure. She learned several alarming facts about PNH, such as childbirth is not recommended, and half of child-bearing mothers do not survive. Those that do survive are given a five to fifteen-year life expectancy.

Instead of allowing these statistics to consume her, Emmie felt God's Presence and the peace He promised. Not only did she and her son, Andrew, survive childbirth (two miracles), but this overcomer recently passed the twenty-seven-year post-diagnosis mark. (Another miracle).

Emmie's refining fire became more intense as she learned about her disease and how it could alter her life. Her years of preparing for a career as an insurance agent were dross being scraped away. Contributing to the family income was not just temporarily scraped away. She's been too fragile to work since her diagnosis. Add in the ongoing agitators of fatigue and migraines. She's been through almost three decades of tests and treatments with no end in sight.

But spend five minutes with Emmie, and you'll quickly notice the refining fire she is still in has not destroyed her. Quite the opposite, in fact. She explained what she's learned from her refining fires: "When I was first diagnosed and my career was scraped away, God showed me my strength would come from Him. I learned He would be sufficient in providing for our needs. I was so focused on our goals and plans for the future before my diagnosis. After my diagnosis, we had to become dependent on Him and trust our future to Him. He also showed me that PNH does not define me. My faith in Him does."

Emmie thanks God for His faithfulness in providing a new medication that gives her a good quality of life. Her son, Andrew, is in grad school while working as a Software Designer. Emmie and her husband, Dennis, love praising and worshipping in the music ministry and serving in the children's ministry at their church.

INTERFERE, IMPEDE, AND SABOTAGE

The purposes of a refining fine are as numerous as the stars in the night sky, but you can be sure God has a unique and specific purpose for each of the refining fires you've experienced. And for those you will encounter in the future. His desire to see His image in you and prove your faith pure and genuine determines the refining fires you will experience.

The challenges you go through may be similar to others (e.g., divorce, financial struggles, health issues, to name a few), but those challenges will be unique in how they are refining *your* specific rough edges. Rough edges. Ugh. We all have them.

As much as you try to hide your rough edges or excuse them or even rationalize why they are just part of who you are, they are dross. Impurities, scum, unwanted material. These unhealthy or sinful habits, quirks, and mannerisms can interfere, impede,  and even sabotage your life. Dross doesn't just impact your goals and dreams. It often impacts your relationships, too. Especially if that dross is interfering, impeding, or sabotaging your relationship with God.

Maybe you see it clearly now. The dots are starting to connect in your mind. While you were in the hottest flame, you lost a relationship, a dream, or a job. Those, too, can be dross if they become idols. Idols? Yes. If your devotion to a relationship, dream, or job surpasses your devotion to God, they are idols. Scraping them away, as painful as it is, recalibrates your heart and mind. You will look more like God as a result.

Describe your rough edges.

How have these rough edges negatively impacted relationships? Caused you to miss out on a promotion, an activity, or reaching a goal?

SIN THAT SEPERATES US FROM GOD

Sometimes the purpose of our refining fire is to convict us of sin in our lives. Sin separates us from God. Additionally, sin impedes or sabotages our goals, dreams, and relationships. Alyssa [G] (a pseudonym to protect her identity) knows this to be true. When her daughter was a year old, she began smoking marijuana with the new man she was dating. She heavily drank every night.

The large amounts of money she made at a gentleman's club funded her drug and alcohol habit. Sadly, her boyfriend's abusiveness increased after they started doing hard drugs together. When Alyssa asked her parents to take care of her daughter, she knew she was choosing an abusive relationship and drugs over her daughter. She'd lost perspective of what was most important. Soon, her daughter's father was given full custody.

By the time her third pregnancy occurred in the four-year relationship with her boyfriend, Alyssa decided she wasn't having another abortion. She stopped drinking and doing drugs. During her pregnancy, her boyfriend left her for her best friend. Dross was being scraped away. After taking a bottle of Ambien and a bottle of Hydrocodone to cope with the betrayal, Alyssa's parents encouraged her to move home. Her son was born soon after.

MADE A LIFE-CHANGING DECISION

A few years later, after a visit with his dad, her son cried all the way home. He said, "I hate you. I want to live with my dad. You are a horrible mother." His words stung, but she knew they were true. She knew she was an alcoholic and a drug addict. Alyssa called his dad and asked him to come get him. Her addiction spiraled out of control. One bad decision led to another. She hit rock bottom.

On the drive to her parents' house, she made a life-changing decision: "If I don't go to rehab, I will die." That decision altered her life in many ways. Clean and sober has been Alyssa's daily choice since graduating from rehab. "Time and again, God convicted me of my sin. I repented several times, only to return to the drugs and alcohol. God had to turn up the heat for me to make a firm and lasting commitment to my sobriety and to Him. I know God forgives me, no matter what. There's no reason possible in human conditions for me to be here except for God. I'm stronger than I ever thought humanly possible."

Alyssa's relationship with her daughter was restored. She and her husband enjoy spending time with their two beautiful children.

Continued sobriety, a loving family, and living healthy give Alyssa reasons to praise God daily.

MATURE AND COMPLETE

Passing through the refining fires that lead to genuine faith can take its toll. Weariness, irritability, frustration, and anger can make us forget God's purpose for the refining fire. This journey you are on is tough. The apostle James points out a character trait we will need when we encounter life's tough challenges, especially when it includes a refining fire.

He said, "Consider it pure joy, my brothers and sisters, whenever you face trials of many kinds, because you know that the testing of your faith produces perseverance. Let perseverance finish its work so that you may be mature and complete, not lacking anything" (James 1:2-4).

Did you notice that the testing of our faith is mentioned again? James said, "the testing of our faith produces perseverance." We need perseverance —the continued effort to do or achieve something despite difficulties, failure, or opposition—to endure the trials of life. When you persevere, you keep moving forward even though your circumstances are difficult. When you persevere, you aren't allowing failure or opposition to stop you. When you persevere, you are flourishing despite the challenges.

When the time comes for God to call you home to the place of abundance—Heaven—your faith will be pure and genuine, and without any impurities or moral imperfections. Your character will look like God's character. Lastly, you will stand before God as a mature, complete, and not lacking anything child of God!

GOD'S VICTORIES IN YOUR LIFE

Whew! You made it to the end of this mile of our journey. Your edges might be crispy. You may smell like smoke. Perhaps your lungs are burning. As hot as those refining fires were, you were never in danger of being destroyed. Nor will you ever be in danger of remaining in the refining fires too long.

You've not been consumed as the enemy promised. You've been refined and are looking more and more like God, just as God promised.

Before you throw your box of matches in your backpack, could we roast some marshmallows by the fire and share stories of God's victories in your life?

God sees himself in the eyes of a refined soul.2

—Robin M. Bertram, author and speaker

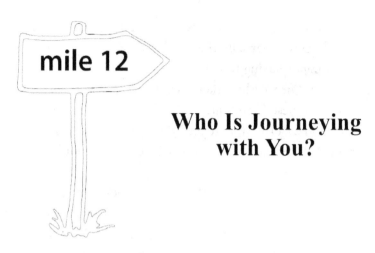

mile 12

Who Is Journeying with You?

Stand side by side as partners in their sufferings. Participate, get into their suffering,

let it make you grimy and tear-stained and drink the draught of communion.1

—Ann Voskamp, author and speaker

Y ou survived the refining fires! Aren't you grateful for the family and friends who encourage us during our seasons of refining fire? As much as we might wish they could be in the cauldron with us, they can't. Refining fire is not a collective experience. Rather, it is an individual one.

The refining you underwent was tailor-made for *you*. During the hottest fire, He scraped away dross that was harming *you*. He kept His eyes on *you* while the flames were developing His character in *you*. Your perseverance is outstanding! The next time you find yourself in a refining fire, remind yourself that you are being refined because *you* are precious and of great value to Him.

As we keep moving forward on our journey, I invited your companions to join us! You could fight life's tough challenges by yourself, but why? I don't believe God intended for you to go it alone. Not just any companions will do. Proverbs 18:24 describes the kinds of companions you

need to journey with you: "But there is a [true, loving] friend who [is reliable and] sticks closer than a brother" (AMP).

Oh, the blessing of having true, loving, and reliable friends. These companions are not fair-weather friends who only come around when life is good. Instead, these friends are invaluable because they love you unconditionally and eagerly support you when you are fighting to overcome challenges. A visual image of two hikers will represent our companions.

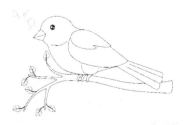

Who are these companions? These friends answer your middle of the night call, ready to listen and talk you through your anxious feelings. And these companions drag you to dinner because you've been hiding for far too long. You can count on these friends to run errands with you, even when you wear your ugliest pajamas. These companions are those loved ones who prepare meals, care for your kids, and take you to doctor's appointments during the toughest days of your challenge. Think these people care for you because they feel obligated? Not a chance. These friends and family truly love you and want to help you as you fight to overcome.

In her book *Sacred Rest*, Dr. Saundra Dalton-Smith defines the time we spend with our companions as social rest. Spending time with your friends is considered rest? Yes! Dr. Dalton-Smith defines social rest as "when we find comfort in our relationships and social interactions" [2] and [finding] "solace in another." [3] Social rest, or time with companions, "comes from being seen, to know someone cared enough to pray for [you] specifically by name," [4] and "reconnects us to uplifting, rewarding relationship exchanges." [5] Lastly, Dr. Saundra explains, "Social rest will increase your sense of belonging and purpose ... improve your self-confidence and self-worth by defeating the lie that you are the only one who feels lonely or unworthy." [6]

Spending time with your companions will revive, nourish, and encourage you when life is going along smoothly. But imagine the significant impact of practicing social rest with your companions when life is hard. Social rest with your friends when you are fighting to overcome is priceless.

Surround the two hikers below with the names of family members, friends, coworkers, and church friends who have supported/are supporting you during your challenge. Don't forget your furry friend(s). We will add more to this image later, so leave space beside each name.

PRODUCTIVE AND HAPPY LIVES

As you read the following overcomer story, look for and highlight the ways Ruby's companions made sure she and her parents never felt alone.

Companions are especially valuable when a child is born with special needs. None of the prenatal tests indicated their child would have neurological struggles, so when Ruby [H] was born, Nicole and Lehr were surprised by the news. Their newborn daughter had Down syndrome. Hours of research gave Nicole hope as she learned people with Down syndrome could lead productive and happy lives.

"Lots of love and support came in every direction," Nicole shared. She and Lehr knew they couldn't navigate this unexpected turn in their path alone. It was Ruby's tribe of family, friends, church friends, and other parents who had children with Down syndrome that encouraged, supported, and strengthened them. Ruby's smile and warm hugs drew even the most curmudgeon person into her circle of companions. Ruby's dad, Lehr, came up with the tagline "Ruby Is a Gem" to unite Ruby's tribe. Excited members of Ruby's tribe donned red t-shirts with the tagline printed on them during the 2014 Buddy Walk for the National Down Syndrome Society.

Ruby's companions interacted with her, hugged her, and did silly things to make her laugh. Her friends stuck closer than a brother, filling Nicole and Lehr with the confidence that they were not raising their child with special needs alone. They didn't wonder how they would make it to all her therapies as many of their companions offered to help. Several insisted on hanging out with Ruby and her siblings, giving Nicole and Lehr the opportunity to have dates and nurture their marriage.

AN UNEXPECTED TURN

When Ruby was two, an unexpected turn intersected their path. Ruby was diagnosed with childhood cancer, specifically acute megakaryoblast leukemia (AML – M7). "It wasn't a hard diagnosis to accept because God prepared us with Ruby's Down syndrome diagnosis. Going through that and seeing how normally she acted weathered us for this next step," Nicole shared. "All I can say is, I felt calm."

Not only did Nicole and Lehr lean hard on their faith during Ruby's leukemia journey, but they also leaned hard on her tribe of companions: those who took care of Ruby's siblings when Ruby had chemo treatments. The ones who brought meals. The friends who covered their family in prayer and believed in Ruby's healing. Those companions who shaved their heads in solidarity with Ruby's balding head. Because each was involved in her life during her fight to overcome leukemia, Ruby's companions joined celebrated her last chemo treatment at her bell-ringing ceremony.

Nicole and Lehr believe all the struggles they have faced since Ruby's birth hold great value. "The blessing of Ruby's cancer was the deepening of my relationship with God. We've gone through these things, so we can help others," Nicole shared. "And I get to encourage and support moms with Down syndrome children and/or children diagnosed with cancer."

READY TO HELP OTHERS

I interviewed Nicole soon after Ruby was in remission. Her words, "We've gone through these things, so we can help others," rang deep. Even though she was weary from months of treatment and uncertainty, she was ready to help others. Ready to encourage and support others. Ready to pass along the comfort she and Lehr received.

Nicole continues to 'walk with' parents who are new to having a special needs child, sharing what she's learned and supporting them on the tough days. Her experiences with Ruby's preschool years and the ongoing fight to ensure Ruby receives the educational services she needs to thrive encourage parents who are beginning the journey with their child.

Dull moments are few and far between at Ruby's house as she loves skateboarding, helping her mom prepare dinner, and earning ice cream treats. Ruby lives life fully just like her nondisabled peers.

Return to the image of the two hikers. Beside each name you listed, describe how he/she comforted, encouraged, or supported you during your challenge.

Use a different color pen to describe how you felt receiving each person's comfort, encouragement, and/or support.

ABOVE AND BEYOND

When you were struggling hard, did someone comfort or encourage you at just the right time? If you've experienced this, I believe she listened to a nudge from the Holy Spirit. Or maybe you received a text that simply said, "Thinking of you today. Keep fighting." Quite possibly, she offered to hang out with your kids so you could nap after work. Perhaps a beautiful bouquet of flowers greeted you at your front door, brightening your mood on the darkest of days. That's God working through your companions. Their comfort and encouragement filled you with the strength to keep going.

Perhaps one specific person comes to mind who you know you couldn't have made it without her during your toughest time. She went above and beyond and served you in ways that nourished your soul. Oh, what a blessing to have these kinds of companions.

I believe this special companion would do it all again because of her love for you. Before this week passes, honor the love, comfort, encouragement, and support she gave you by writing a note or calling her to say thank you.

SO THAT

When I think of these kinds of companions, I'm reminded of a comparison Kristi McClelland shared in her *Jesus & Women* Bible study. She said, "We want to live like rivers, not lakes. We want the Word to travel to us, through us, to others. We have truly learned a thing when we can give it away." [7] Rivers flow freely and move in a specific direction. Lakes, on the other hand, are contained bodies of water that lack flowing water.

Second Corinthians 1:3-4 says, "Blessed [gratefully praised and adored] be the God and Father of our Lord Jesus Christ, the Father of mercies and the God of all comfort, who comforts and encourages us in every trouble so that we will be able to comfort and encourage those who are in any kind of trouble, with the comfort with which we ourselves are comforted by God" (AMPC).

Please highlight 'so that' in the preceding verses.

If we use Kristi's comparison, these verses do not advocate a 'lake' mindset. Instead, verse 3 reminds you that God filled you with comfort and encouragement during your troubles. On your hard days, on the days you thought you wouldn't survive, and on the days you wanted to give up—*so that*—you could be a river. And, in turn, you can comfort and encourage others who are struggling.

Now, use a blue crayon or blue colored pencil to draw a river above 'the God of all comfort, who comforts and encourages us in every trouble.' Now, draw another river above 'we will be able to comfort and encourage those who are in any kind of trouble, with the comfort with which we ourselves are comforted by God.' Make sure each side of the river connects to the highlighted 'so that.'

Spend a few minutes looking at the river you drew above these verses. What thoughts or feelings come to mind?

Nicole couldn't be a lake after all the comfort, encouragement, and support she, Lehr, and Ruby received. Instead, the comfort, encouragement, and support that flowed into her now flows freely into many, many others.

Are you being a river? If so, keep flowing! If not, it's time to move in the direction of another who needs comfort, encouragement, and support. Let your loving comfort, generous encouragement, and steadfast support flow freely. Breathe life and strength into others. Share the courage you've gained. Lean in and listen. Give big hugs to those who are struggling.

Now is the time to follow through with your *so that*. You likely know of one or more people who are struggling. List his or her name below. Beside each name, describe the encouragement, comfort, or support you can give and when you will give it.

FRONT-LINE CAREGIVER

Caregiving is a beautiful way to be a river to someone who is fighting for his or her life. Aimee [1] never hesitated when the time came to be her sister, Tracy's, front-line caregiver. You might remember Tracy's story from mile 03 in *Challenges Won't Stop Me*.

"From the moment we heard Tracy's diagnosis of stomach cancer, I went into caregiver mode. It wasn't a decision I had to mull over. I just did what I did because I loved Tracy. I knew we were in a fight for Tracy's life, hoping for the best and preparing for the worst," Aimee shared. The words "4% survival rate" when Tracy was diagnosed didn't deter Aimee. Suffering, pain, grief, and death were all likely. Like a river, Aimee poured generously into her sister. Because she believes in Proverbs 17:17, which says, "A friend loves at all times, and a brother is born for a time of adversity."

Within a few days of Tracy's diagnosis, the most unimaginable and beautiful thing happened. Tracy's sorority sisters, co-workers, friends, and family came together as Team Tracy. "It was that and more to me," Aimee shared. "I knew I wouldn't be alone in giving care for Tracy."

Team Tracy was Tracy *and* Aimee's tribe. Tracy benefitted greatly from each person's unique gift of love, strength, and prayers. And Aimee benefitted from others on the team who helped with Tracy's needs when she had to work or care for her family. "Offering encouragement and reminding Tracie of how richly she was blessed and would ultimately be in Heaven was of utmost importance to me. I stressed how her fight against stomach cancer would impact so many people because they saw her contagious smile, her grit and determination, and her will to live despite all the suffering," Aimee shared.

THE CORE IS NEVER STANDING ALONE

 Aimee described her role and that of Team Tracy as a beautiful and delicate flower: "At the center of a daisy is a detailed and beautiful core. Unseen are all the interconnected petals encircling the core before it blooms. When the daisy blooms, the core is never standing alone, but is connected to all the petals. I knew Tracy was the core. And I was one of the many, many petals of Team Tracy. We were all encircling her and caring for her. I may have been the front-line caregiver, but I could not have done any of it without all the other interconnected petals of Team Tracy."

Team Tracy comforted and encouraged Tracy throughout her four-year battle, which included two recurrences of stomach cancer. After Tracy's passing, Aimee shared, "Someday you may be that front-line caregiver, facing the enemy head-on. Or maybe you'll be the core of the daisy. Either way, expect love, miracles, bonding, friendships, restoration, selflessness, unconditional support, and unseen blessings. God is bigger than any statistic, and there is joy in the suffering."

Aunt Aimee continues to pour into the lives of Tracy's children. She is passionate about helping rescue dogs find their forever homes and helping clients restore their health. She and her husband, James, enjoy being active with their kids.

Maybe the role of caregiver frightens you as you aren't sure how you'll handle their suffering or care for their needs. Or maybe your demanding career leaves little time to assume such a big responsibility. What ways could you help the person who is the front-line caregiver for someone you know and love?

VEERED OFF THE RIGHT PATH

Companions aren't limited to those who have meals delivered to your house or who cut your overgrown lawn while you're in the hospital. While those acts of service are helpful and show their love for you, you may need a different type of love. What if you and I need a companion who knows us well and loves us unconditionally to look us in the eye and call out our sin? Oh boy. Yep, I'm going there.

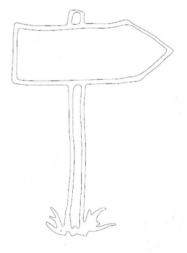

It happened when you veered off the right path into dangerous territory. You didn't see the danger. Or maybe you were choosing to ignore the red flags warning you to go no further. You may not have seen those warnings, but your companion does. She knows if you don't turn back now, you are heading straight into destruction.

When you're heading down dangerous paths, you need companions who will be firm, direct, *and* loving. Redirecting you back to the right path is risky. Well-meaning words could end the friendship. These friends willingly take that risk because they believe your life is worth it. These kinds of companions are the rarest form of love.

King David was described as a man after God's own heart (1 Samuel 13:14 and Acts 13:22), yet he's the same man who veered off the right path when he summoned another man's wife. Lust tainted his vision. He ignored the red flags and slept with Bathsheba. The result? A child was conceived. Instead of repenting, seeking forgiveness, or asking God for guidance in this situation, David took matters into his own hands.

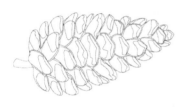

David summoned Bathsheba's husband, Uriah, and asked, "Haven't you just come from a military campaign? Why didn't you go home?" (2 Samuel 11:10). If Uriah had slept with his wife while on military leave, David believed his predicament would be solved. Instead, Uriah replied, "The ark and Israel and Judah are staying in tents, and my commander Joab and my lord's men are camped in the open country. How could I go to my house to eat and drink and make love to my wife? As surely as you live, I will not do such a thing" (2 Samuel 11:11).

Uriah's integrity was an unexpected obstacle in David's plan. Already wading neck deep in dangerous territory, David set another plan in motion. He was firm in his desire to have what wasn't his. Putting Uriah on the front lines so he would be killed in battle would solve David's problem, right? No. Not in God's eyes: "But the thing David had done displeased the LORD" (2 Samuel 11:27).

SIN SEPARATED HIM FROM GOD

Thankfully, one of David's closest and trusted friends was willing to risk their friendship to keep him from continuing down a dangerous path. When he heard about David's actions, Nathan approached him in a firm, direct, and loving way. As a prophet, Nathan knew his actions weren't just poor choices, David's sins separated him from God.

In 2 Samuel 12, Nathan told David a parable in which one man prepared his neighbor's lamb for a traveler instead of preparing his own lamb. "David burned with anger against the man and said to Nathan, "As surely as the LORD lives, the man who did this must die! He must pay for that lamb four times over, because he did such a thing and had no pity" (2 Samuel 12: 1-6).

Nathan knew his next words could end their friendship, yet he boldly said, "You are the man! This is what the LORD, the God of Israel, says: 'I anointed you king over Israel, and I delivered you from the hand of Saul. I gave your master's house to you, and your master's wives into your arms. I gave you all Israel and Judah. And if all this had been too little, I would have given you even more. Why did you despise the word of the LORD by doing what is evil in his eyes? You struck down Uriah the Hittite with the sword and took his wife to be your own. You killed him with the sword of the Ammonites. Now, therefore, the sword will never depart from your house, because you despised me and took the wife of Uriah the Hittite to be your own'" (2 Samuel 12:7-10).

Nathan's words pierced David's heart. He confessed, "I have sinned against the LORD" (2 Samuel 12:13). David's confession restored his relationship with God; however, the consequence was almost unbearable. After Nathan left, the LORD struck David's son with an illness. Fasting and worshipping day and night, David pleaded with God to heal his son's illness. Sadly, his son died on the seventh day.

Proverbs 27:17 says, "As iron sharpens iron, so one person sharpens another." Not only did Nathan's convicting parable led David to repent, but his words also sharpened—to make more acute, intense, or effective—David for the latter half of his reign as king of Judah.

If you've had a companion like Nathan, who risked your friendship to redirect you back to the right path, describe the conversation and how you felt about his or her words. Did the friendship survive?

ONE ANOTHER

Our relationship with Jesus is our foundation. We most assuredly need Him during every challenge we face, but He knew we would also need others. Oh, how David needed his companion, Nathan. Jesus taught how we are to care for and love those who are our companions in what are known as the 'one another' verses. Fifty-nine 'one another' verses can be found in the New Testament.

The following fifteen verses cover the main themes of Jesus' 'one another' message. Please write these verses using your preferred version of Scripture. If you don't have a preferred version, go to bible-hub.com. Type in a verse, then scroll down to read the different translations. Choose one that will help you remember the concept.

Mark 9:50

John 13:34

John 15:12-13

Romans 12:10

Galatians 5:13

Galatians 6:2

Ephesians 4:2

Ephesians 4:32

Colossians 3:13

1 Thessalonians 3:12

1 Thessalonians 5:11

Hebrews 10:24-25

James 5:16

1 Peter 5:5

1 John 4:11

Highlight just the 'one another' phrase in each verse.

How are your companions fulfilling these 'one another' verses in your life? List his or her name beside the applicable verse.

Remember the *so that* part of 2 Corinthians 1:3-4? How are you fulfilling these 'one another' verses in your companions' lives?

AN IMPORTANT PART OF YOUR JOURNEY

When I think about the 'one another' verses, I'm reminded of how important we are to one another. Without question, your companions are an integral part of your journey. Yes, you could make it without them. But why? They add laughter, encouragement, and a shoulder to cry on. And they remind you to keep fighting. Cherish these special people.

Even though you might want to hide your companions in your backpack for the rest of our journey, it's not possible. Put a sunflower in your backpack instead. A sunflower symbolizes friendship, loyalty, resilience, endurance, and hope.

Each time you see a sunflower, may it remind you of how blessed you are to have such wonderful companions in your life. It's time to journey on!

A friend is someone who helps you up when you are down, and if they can't, they lay down

beside you and listen.8

—Winnie the Pooh

mile 13

Are Your Fears and Enemies Poisoning You?

Fear is Satan's favorite tool to use to torment people.1

—Joyce Meyer, author and speaker

The universal poison control number is 1-800-222-1222. When would you need this number? You would need it anytime you suspect a poisoning from medications, carbon monoxide, cleaning products, a jellyfish sting, swallowed batteries, ingested poisonous berries, spider bites, ingested gasoline, inhaled aerosol sprays, or a snake bite. The exhaustive list of substances on the Poison Control website of things that can poison us is quite overwhelming.

You may be wondering why I'm going into such detail about poison. Just a quick look at how *Merriam-Webster* defines *poison*, and you'll understand. *Poison* is "a substance that usually kills, injures, or impairs an organism; something destructive or harmful; to exert a baneful influence on; corrupt; to inhibit the activity, course, or occurrence of."

I bet you can easily think of a handful of people, emotions, and circumstances that are poisonous to you. Unfortunately, we must traverse an area known to have a large snake population. I've scouted other trails, looking for any alternate routes. We must go through here to get to our destination. Keep the Poison Control number handy as we travel this mile. And be strong and courageous!

For those who like snakes, aren't afraid to hold snakes, and don't avoid nature walks during snake season, this mile of our journey might not be as painful for you as it is for the rest of us. You are indeed a unique human. To me, a snake is a snake is a snake. Therefore, every snake is an enemy. Additionally, snakes fill me with fear. Lots and lots of fear.

Suppose a chainsaw roared near you. A snake hissing next to your feet would seize your attention. You should back away slowly. Most snakes will strike when provoked. If one bites you, its poison will quickly reach your bloodstream, causing labored breathing, disturbed vision, numbness, and severe pain. In extreme cases, death occurs.

Our fears and enemies hiss, strike, and bite. When they do, you might experience a rising heart rate, labored breathing, and disturbed vision.  Rather than physical numbness and pain, their bite *numbs your emotions and fills your heart with pain*. Because our fears and enemies behave similarly to snakes, the visual image for fears and enemies is a snake. Don't worry. I won't be asking you to put a snake in your backpack at the end of this mile!

FELL PREY TO HIS LIES

Introduced in Genesis 3, the crafty serpent tempted Eve to eat fruit from the tree of life. He approached Eve and hissed, "Did God really say, 'You must not eat from any tree in the garden?'" (Genesis 3:1). Eve replied, "We may eat fruit from the trees in the garden, but God did say, 'You must not eat fruit from the tree that is in the middle of the garden, and you must not touch it, or you will die'" (Genesis 3:2-3). Because Eve responded to the serpent's hiss, his plan progressed to a strike. A strike filled with lies: "You will not certainly die. For God knows that when you eat from it your eyes will be opened, and you will be like God, knowing good and evil" (Genesis 3:4-5).

Eve *fell prey to his lies*, believing the fruit was good for food and pleasing to the eye. *He convinced* Eve the fruit was also desirable for gaining wisdom. She took a bite of the fruit from the forbidden tree. When Eve bit the fruit and gave it to Adam, the serpent effectively bit both of them. *Poison, also known as sin, was thrust into their hearts.*

Throughout Scripture, the serpent is also known as the enemy, adversary, devil, prince of the dark, and Satan. Adam and Eve's story exemplifies the enemy's three goals: *to kill, steal, and destroy* (John 10:10). He will use strategies, deceptions, and schemes to accomplish these goals. We cannot be unaware of his schemes (2 Corinthians 2:11).

REAL OR PERCEIVED DANGER

Two of Satan's most effective strategies are *deceiving or manipulating you with fear and strategically placing an enemy in your life.*

Fear—a threat of real or perceived danger—*heightens all your senses to levels that are difficult to calm. Dread, uneasiness, agitation, worry, and/or apprehension consume your mind. Not knowing when or where or how the real or perceived danger will strike amplifies those emotions.* Your mind begins *unraveling worst-case scenarios,* convincing you that defeat, failure, or death are the inevitable outcomes of your challenge. Your body can't differentiate between real or perceived danger. Thus, the clammy hands, the racing heart, and the clenched jaw.

Satan studies your words and actions to determine how to inject fear into your life. Who or what *upsets you?* Who or what *makes you cower?* What do want to do that you say "No" to because *you are afraid?* He takes note of your responses and *waits for an opportune time* (Luke 4:13). When the devil sees the perfect opportunity to *deceive or manipulate you,* he *strikes you with fear where it will hurt you the most.*

A relationship you hoped would progress suddenly ends. Our adversary strikes with the intent of *tricking you into believing you are not worthy of friendship or love.* Just when you resolve to turn your life around, he will *threaten to expose your bad choices and amp up the shame you already feel.* Maybe you realize you're sliding into the comparison trap. The enemy eagerly *incites you to be jealous of anoth-*

er's success. He won't stop there. He will *overwhelm you with a fear of not measuring up. Of not being enough.* Perhaps you invested time, energy, and money into following your dreams, but obstacle after obstacle blocked your way. Satan will *taunt you with the ridicule your friends and family will heap on you when you fail.* How will you ever recover?

Briefly describe a time when you experienced fear or perceived danger. What thoughts raced through your mind?

How did your body respond?

IMPACTS HER LIFE EVERY SINGLE DAY

When I shared Niki's [J] story years ago, I explained my phobia of snakes, called ophidiophobia, as being mostly avoidable. And I pointed out that some phobias are not. Unfortunately, Niki's phobia is unavoidable, impacting every single day of her life. Some, like Niki, cringe at the idea of interacting socially. Physical manifestations of sweaty palms, a racing heartbeat, and/or a churning stomach collide with their fear. Because social interactions occur almost everywhere we go—work, the grocery store, their child's school, and restaurants—social phobias induce anxiety. *Sometimes, the fear is so great, it causes panic.*

Niki grew up in a household of adults where the tried-and-true motto of 'children should be seen but not heard' rang true. Raised by her grandfather, she spent much time alone, entertaining herself, while all the adults talked. She wasn't taught how to initiate or carry on a conversation. As a young adult, she was diagnosed with social anxiety disorder. This diagnosis gave a name to all the fears she held inside.

PREPARE FOR THE ENEMY'S ATTACKS

When she was a child, *no one helped Niki prepare to face her fears.* As her faith grew, she decided she needed to prepare for the enemy's attacks. Niki pulled out her map and found verses that would fill her with courage. Every time Niki knows she will be in a social situation, she says the following verses out loud: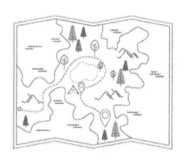

- "The Lord is with me; I will not be afraid. What can man do to me?" (Psalm 118:6)
- "If God is for us, who can be against us?" (Romans 8:31)
- "So do not fear, for I am with you; do not be dismayed, for I am your God. I will strengthen and help you; I will uphold you with my righteous right hand" (Isaiah 41:10).

Do these verses eliminate her social anxiety every time she encounters a social situation? Unfortunately, no. But, when fighting those fears, she maximizes her counterattack by striking with fear's weakness: God. The enemy is weakened when Niki speaks those verses aloud, which gives her the courage to interact socially.

For many years, Niki didn't know her purpose. With her multi-purpose tool of prayer by her side, she brought her concerns before God: "I have no social skills, so how am I supposed to serve you if I spend most, if not all, of my time alone?" God answered her prayer in an unexpected way. One of Niki's close friends suddenly passed away, leaving her five children without a parent.

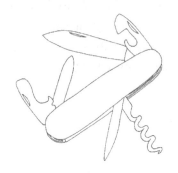

God prompted Niki to face her social fears by adopting and loving those children. She explained, "To raise young children, you must be an example of kindness, acceptance, and love. I needed patience with myself when meeting teachers, the parents of their friends, and joining the PTA. I realized it takes practice to build social skills. Not only do I have my purpose now, but I also have more than my share of loved ones surrounding me every day."

Accepting a supervisory role at work and becoming an activity art leader at a nursing home gave Niki even more opportunities to strengthen her social skills. When she compares who she was before her friend's untimely death to who she is now, she confidently says, "The changes in me would have never been possible without my faith in God. There is no doubt He lives in me."

YOU HAVE ENEMIES

Left unchecked and unaddressed, fears can *poison you. Paralyze you. Stop you.* Enemies can too. Perhaps you're thinking, *I don't have any enemies.* Your enemies might not be a giant who *mocks you* and your God (1 Samuel 17:8). Your enemies might not be a Judas who *sells you out* (Matthew 26:15). And your enemies might not be a king who *pursues you with the intent to kill you* (1 Samuel 23:7-24:22). However, your enemy might be one of the other nearly four hundred 'enemy' or 'enemies' mentioned in Scripture. Be assured, my friend, you have enemies.

Enemies by their very nature are *antagonistic*. Satan strategically inserts enemies into your life to *cause conflict, obstruct your goals, place irresistible temptations in your path, bully you, spread lies about you, encourage you to forsake your morals and values, and persuade you to live in defeat, or worse, to give up*. An enemy's goals are to *sidetrack you, push you beyond your limits, cause you to question your beliefs, embarrass you, and ruin your reputation*. Recognize your enemies now?

Describe any antagonists/enemies who oppose you.

How are you responding?

A STRONG HOLD ON YOU

Like snakes, your fears and enemies *slither in and out of your life, waiting for the perfect time to strike.* King David's enemies struck frequently. Wanting protection and quiet time with the LORD, David often retreated to strongholds—a fortified, inaccessible, and not easily penetrated place; a place of security or survival—in the desert. These forts and caves were places of protection. After successful battles, David praised God for being his stronghold: "He is my stronghold, my refuge and my savior—from violent people you save me" (2 Samuel 22:3). God is your fortified, inaccessible (to Satan), and impenetrable stronghold.

Isn't it just like the enemy though to 'flip the script' on us by creating spiritual strongholds? *Unhealthy, destructive, or sinful behaviors that we make inaccessible, impenetrable, and protect at all costs* are spiritual strongholds. In a devotional about strongholds, Max Lucado asks, "Where does the devil have a stronghold on you? Ahh, there is the word that fits–stronghold–fortress, citadel, thick walls, tall gates. It's as if the devil has *fenced in one negative attribute, one bad habit, one weakness and constructed a rampart around it.*" [2] Pornography, addiction, cheating on your spouse, and gluttony are just a few of the ways the enemy has a strong hold on you. Because Satan *wants you to stay trapped in the thing that has a strong hold on you, he increases its pull on you,* so you refuse to admit your stronghold is destroying you.

Like a boa constrictor, your strongholds will *coil around you, squeeze hard enough to stop your blood from flowing,* and then *devour you.* Very likely, *you won't feel you are being devoured* by your stronghold. Constricting and ingesting prey is a time-consuming process. Elizabeth Brainerd, a biologist at Brown University, explains, "They [boa constrictors] do this for 10, 15, up to 45 minutes." [3] *The enemy is patient. Your destruction will happen slowly over time.*

Strongholds aren't limited to destructive behaviors. Emotional strongholds, such as jealousy, bitterness, unforgiveness, pride, a judgmental attitude, anger, and greed will *cripple you* as fast as a venomous snake bite. Vipers "don't always have the most deadly bites, but they have *the most painful ones* ... The key to the excruciating pain of the viper's bite is its tissue-destroying venom, which dissolves cell walls and causes internal bleeding. *As the venom works its way through the body, so does the pain.*" [4]

Are you fiercely guarding and protecting your spiritual strongholds? Refusing to turn away from them? At some point, the painful and deadly outcomes of boas and vipers could happen to you.

Describe any behavioral/emotional strongholds in your life.

How are they squeezing the life out of you? Causing you excruciating pain?

UNGUARDED, UNAWARE, AND UNPREPARED

Your greatest enemy is Satan. Never let that fact be watered down, dismissed, or pushed to the back of your mind. *He is not casually waiting for an opportunity to attack you.* First Peter 5:8 warns us, "Your enemy the devil *prowls around like a roaring lion looking for someone to devour.*"

Underline *looking for someone to devour.*

Merriam-Webster defines *devour* as "to eat up greedily or ravenously; to use up or destroy as if by eating; and to prey upon." Satan is *looking for someone who is unguarded, unaware, and unprepared. He is purposeful in who he attacks. He's looking for the easiest prey.* The enemy keeps his eyes on the one he can easily attack with fears and enemies, *knowing she won't fight back.* Satan will greedily and ravenously destroy you. And enjoy it. His intended outcome is not to just leave bite marks or scratches. *His ultimate intention is to devour you.*

Underline *unguarded, unaware, unprepared, easiest prey,* and *won't fight back* in the previous paragraph.

Those words or phrases describe the type of person Satan is looking for to devour. Do any of those words or phrases describe you?

How do you avoid being devoured? Two ways. First, you must follow the motto of the Scouts: "Be prepared." Consistently using your essential gear, including your carabiner, is excellent preparation. However, Satan studies you intently, looking for a millimeter or more of unfortified space in your mind or heart. He is so cunning, so manipulative, and so evil that being prepared won't always be enough.

MUST BE STRATEGIC

The second way you can avoid being devoured is by *always being* ready to counterattack. The enemy *isn't just toying with you.* This is all out war. As strategic as Satan is, you, too, must be strategic. How? You must learn Satan's strengths and weaknesses.

The serpent's strengths are the numerous ways he manipulates fears and enemies to steal, kill, and destroy you. You've seen his strengths already; you just might not have realized it.

Excluding *Merriam-Webster*, the italicized words and phrases throughout this mile are the enemy's strengths.

Grab a highlighter, flip back to the beginning of this mile, and highlight all the italicized words or phrases.

Because you and I might not bow to the enemy's schemes the first time or two we encounter them, **please highlight *persistence* as one of the enemy's strengths.**

While this list doesn't fully encompass all Satan's strengths, describe the feelings that arise when you think about him strategically enacting these in your life.

As calculated and strategic as Satan's strengths might be, he does have a weakness. His weakness is God. And everything and everyone connected to God.

Let's consider all the ways you can counterattack the enemy. Expressing your love for God with your faith, your prayers, your acceptance of God's forgiveness, your unwavering hope, your trust, your reliance on God, and your joy are actions that weaken the enemy's power.

When you study God's Word and live it out, extend forgiveness, show mercy and grace, are obedient, show kindness, express gratitude, turn the other cheek instead of retaliating, love unconditionally, praise and worship God, live in peace despite the chaos, serve others, proclaim Heaven as your eternal home, and point others to God, Satan's power is weakened. Essentially, when your relationship with God is active and vibrant, all the enemy can see is God. God living powerfully in you. The enemy has no choice but to slither away.

A PEP TALK FROM GOD

God's chosen people encountered snakes (fears and enemies) during their forty years in the wilderness.

> Fears: drowning while walking through the parted Red Sea, going hungry and thirsty, being abandoned by God, being attacked and killed, and never reaching the Promised Land.

> Enemies: Egyptians, Amalekites, Canaanites, Moabites, Midianites, Amorites, Jebusites, Hittites, Perizzites, Gibeonites, Hivites, and Jebusites.

When God passed the baton from Moses to Joshua, He knew Satan would antagonize/bully/obstruct Joshua with fears and enemies. In Joshua 1:5-9, God gave Joshua a peptalk to fortify him for the tasks and responsibilities ahead.

God said, "No one will be able to stand against you all the days of your life. As I was with Moses, so I will be with you: I will never leave you nor forsake you. Be strong and courageous, because you will lead these people to inherit the land I swore to their ancestors to give them. Be strong and very courageous. Be careful to obey all the law my servant Moses gave you; do not turn from it to the right or to the left, that you may be successful wherever you go. Keep this Book of the Law always on your lips; meditate on it day and night, so that you may be careful to do everything written in it. Then you will be prosperous and successful. Have I not commanded you? Be strong and courageous. Do not be afraid; do not be discouraged, for the LORD your God will be with you wherever you go."

Underline the following five phrases in the previous verses: 'no one will be able to stand against you,' 'I will be with you,' 'I will never leave you nor forsake you,' 'you may be successful wherever you go,' and 'the LORD your God will be with you wherever you go.'

These phrases weren't just spoken to Joshua. They apply to you, as well. Write the phrase which encourages you most and describe why.

Reread the verses in Joshua 1 and highlight the three times 'strong and courageous' appear. Use a different color highlighter than the one you used for the enemy's strengths.

The words *strong* and *courageous* in Joshua chapter 1 made me pause. *Merriam-Webster* defines *strong* as "having, showing, or able to exert great bodily or muscular power; physically vigorous or robust; and mentally powerful or vigorous and of great moral power, firmness, or courage." *Courage* means "mental or moral strength to venture, persevere, and to withstand danger, fear, or difficulty."

In the paragraph above, highlight the parts of the definitions for *strong* and *courageous* that fill you with boldness to face your fears and enemies.

If being *strong* and *courageous* when facing challenges is difficult for you, go to biblegateway.com, type in 'strong and courageous,' and highlight those eleven verses in your Bible.

God said, "As I was with Moses, so I will be with you." Personalize this statement by filling in the blank below with the name of the Bible character or person who inspires you because of the great odds he or she faced and overcame.

As I (God) was with _____, so I will be with *YOU*; I will never leave *YOU* nor forsake *YOU*."

Now, replace your name above the three instances of YOU.

PLACED IN FOSTER CARE

Teres'sa K felt fear every time she encountered her enemies. These were the worst kind of enemies: the people who were supposed to love and protect her. At the tender age of five, Teres'sa's grandfather fondled her and made her touch him. Not too long after that, her father was killed in a truck accident and her mother was arrested for prostitution.

With no one to take care of her and her younger sister, they were placed in foster care. Both she and her younger sister were eventually adopted. Malnourished, not taken care of, not provided adequate clothing, and feeling scared all the time are just a few of the words Teres'sa used to describe this new family environment.

Within eight months of their adoption, sexual abuse started. Teres'sa remembers her adopted father saying, "This is how we show love. This is the way a man shows a woman love." The feel and the smell of this love couldn't be scrubbed away, leaving Teres'sa feeling filthy and ugly. His abuse occurred as a punishment and as a reward. "If we made our parents mad, they would punish us by physically and sexually abusing us. If we did something right, they would abuse us as a reward. If we wanted to go somewhere or buy something, the abuse would be the means of getting it. It was very confusing."

Teres'sa became pregnant by her adopted father when she was sixteen. A forced dating relationship began with a twenty-one-year-old man. Explicit instructions were given to have sex, so they could get married and claim the baby was his. When Teres'sa and the man refused to comply, her father beat her in the stomach, causing a miscarriage. Teres'sa's enemies were relentless in trying to devour her.

DIDN'T KNOW HOW TO FIGHT BACK

Teres'sa snuck around with Ken (a pseudonym to protect his identity) when she was seventeen, which led to running away from home and getting married at eighteen. Four years later, a beautiful daughter was born. Soon after her daughter was born, Ken began abusing drugs and became controlling. He felt Teres'sa was giving their daughter more attention than him and treating him as if he didn't exist. She would disassociate when she was being physically beaten as she didn't know how to fight back.

Teres'sa endured Ken's abuse for six years before ending their marriage. Over the next fourteen years, Teres'sa remained single. Then, she met Steve (a pseudonym to protect his identity) and became pregnant with her second daughter. They did not stay together. Because she still hadn't dealt with the abuse or her PTSD, Teres'sa spun into a deep depression and attempted suicide several times.

Multiple fears and multiple enemies attacked Teres'sa for decades. Knowing it was time to stop the terror, she counterattacked the attacks by seeking counseling at a crisis intervention center. Confronting the parents who adopted her didn't erase the memories of abuse, pain, and trauma. Forgiving them freed her, which allowed her to move on with her life.

Teres'sa came to the realization that God allowed those horrible years of abuse, so she could help other women who've been abused. Helping others gave her a new path in life.

Since that time, Teres'sa has counseled and mentored hundreds of women who have been sexually abused.

The good God had in mind when those atrocities were happening in Teres'sa's life can be seen when women at The Shafer Center hear her journey of overcoming and know they are not alone. Listening, comforting, and encouraging women who share their pain and shame—just one of the ways Teres'sa impacts countless lives.

Additionally, Teres'sa boldly declared she would not allow abuse to impact the lives of her daughters or grandchildren. As such, she showers them with love. A close relationship with each of them fills her with joy.

GOD INTENDED IT FOR GOOD

Maybe like me, you are frazzled and emotionally spent after focusing on our fears and enemies while we walked this mile. Not to mention all the snake references. I hear you pleading, "It's time to leave this snake-infested land!" I agree.

Before we move on to mile 14, Genesis 50:20 will help us understand why we must go through difficult challenges. This verse says, "You intended to harm me, but God intended it for good to accomplish what is now being done, the saving of many lives." The combination of these words is hard to reconcile. In the ways of the world, God working the things meant to harm us into our good just doesn't make sense.

These unbelievable words were spoken by Joseph, a man who faced many difficult and harmful situations. Joseph's brothers sold him into slavery. He was imprisoned even though he didn't commit any crimes. While serving as second in command, Joseph was seduced by Pharoah's wife. When he refused her advances, she falsely accused him of sleeping with her. No matter which way Joseph turned, fears and enemies stood like sentinels in his path (Genesis 37-50). He could have cowered to their hisses, strikes, and bites. But he didn't.

When Joseph's enemies and fears persevered in their attempts to destroy him, he could have quit following God. Instead, he "[was] assured and knew that [God being a partner in his labor] all things work together and are [fitting into a plan] for good and to those who love God and are called according to [His] design and purpose" (Romans 8:28, AMPC).

Every fear you've felt and every enemy you've encountered will be used by God to accomplish good in your life. Just like He did in Niki's and Teres'sa's lives. Will you see that good right away? Not likely. More than a decade elapsed between the time Joseph's brothers sold him into slavery and when he said those powerful words in Genesis 50:20. In between, Joseph spent ten years in prison, which to some would seem like wasted time. Not to Joseph.

He took advantage of the silence and solitude to draw closer to God. And God took advantage of that time to build Joseph's leadership skills and impart wisdom that would save his country from famine. Joseph feared for his life when Potiphar's wife seduced him, but that experience solidified his integrity and his obedience to God's Word. God used every fear and every attack Joseph encountered as fuel for His purpose: the saving of many lives.

OPPORTUNITY TO GROW

If fears and enemies aren't assaulting you right now, you might be able to see how they provided opportunities for you to grow. On the other hand, if you're still being taunted by fears or harassed by enemies, it might be difficult to see the good yet.

Whichever place you are in right now, consider how strength was built when you did not allow fears to poison you or enemies to overpower you. The repetitive hissing of your fears made you weary, but you didn't give up. Instead, you gained perseverance. Compassion was cultivated when enemies showed indifference or hatred toward you. You loved and extended empathy in return. When you confidently stood up to the bullies known as fears and enemies, courage and grit began coursing through you like a rushing river.

When you learned valuable life lessons from each fear or enemy, you gained wisdom. When it seemed as if no good outcome could result from all the vicious attacks from enemies, your faith grew. You realized you are living proof of God's goodness in your life. The good God planned for you are strong branches called strength, perseverance, compassion, empathy, courage, grit, wisdom, and faith.

Because you prepared for and counterattacked when fears and enemies attacked, God developed the qualities and attributes mentioned in the previous paragraphs in you to accomplish His plan for your life. And I assert there is another benefit—one that is immeasurable in its value. What if fighting your fears and enemies was an opportunity for you to grow stronger and deeper roots in your understanding of God? Praise God for all the ways our fears and enemies allow Him to accomplish growth in our lives!

Describe the ways you've grown from the fears and enemies you've encountered.

EQUIPPED TO FIGHT

It's finally time to leave this snake-infested land! And not a moment too soon! As challenging as this mile proved to be, we sometimes forget how cunning and strategic Satan is. He will continue to attack you, so be prepared for those snakes. When—not if, but when— the devil attacks, immediately counterattack with his weakness: God. You are equipped and empowered to fight, my strong and courageous friend!

I wouldn't put a snake in my backpack! Nor would I encourage you to do so. Instead, copy Poison Control's number on cardstock and toss it in your backpack. Pull it out every time fears and/or enemies attack. Believe God will protect you and fight for you. With those truths living in your mind and heart, confidently keep moving forward!

> You cannot defeat an enemy you do not admit exists.[5]
>
> —Army lieutenant general Michael T. Flynn

mile 14

How Are You Treating
Your Illnesses and Injuries?

A healthy body is a guest-chamber for the soul; a sick body is a prison.1

—Philosopher Francis Bacon

That last mile with all those snakes was an E-X-T-R-A lengthy mile, wasn't it? I'm running full speed into this one. And I feel you right on my heels. Fighting our fears and enemies is demanding work, leaving us mentally, emotionally, and physically wounded and battered. Those refining fires may have been a couple of miles back, but I'm still feeling a little charred. Are you? I'm so grateful first aid is available for those of us who need it.

Before your current challenge intersected your path, thrusting you into a journey you weren't expecting to take, your thoughts, emotions, and body may have been in excellent health. But not anymore. Your body, though intricately woven by God, is fallible. Wounds, bruises, or maybe even scars document the hits your body has taken.

Bones break. Diseases invade and assume control. Viruses bump and knock through our bodies like trains speeding through a dark tunnel. Cancer ravages and destroys healthy cells. When these challenges intersect our path, we cry out for physical healing.

Healing isn't only reserved for your physical body though. Emotional, financial, spiritual, mental, and relational illnesses and injuries also need God's healing. Healing is needed for a broken heart after a failed marriage. Or for canyon deep wounds from a parent who thinks their child is never good enough. A bank account that is depleted from habitually spending money you don't have needs financial healing. Maybe the healing you need is to fill the indescribable void after a loved one has passed away.

While it's invisible to others, you may need healing from the relentless anxiety attacks that have sucked the life out of you. Or it could be that you need God's forgiveness to heal the shame you carry from years of making poor decisions. God's healing can be found in every one of these situations. A first aid kit is an obvious visual image to represent your healing.

What area(s) of your life need healing? Be specific with your description(s).

MAN-MADE MEDICATIONS AND TREATMENTS

As much as I prefer natural healing, such as chiropractic care, acupuncture, and whole food supplements, I have immense respect and gratitude for the man-made medications and treatments I've received over the years to treat my neurological struggles. I'm amazed a tiny white pill taken at the first inkling of a migraine stops the excruciating pain in my head almost immediately.

Not long ago, I shared my brain surgery story with a new friend. After listening to my journey, she said, "It's unbelievable to think your neurosurgeon took a healthy blood vessel from one side of your brain and grafted it into the other side to encourage good blood flow." I'm the first to admit it is still shocking to hear my miracle described. Then I replied, "Yeah, it really is unbelievable. I am forever grateful to God. And I'm grateful for Dr. Khaldi, my brilliant neurosurgeon, who shared the gifts and talents God gave him to heal me."

While medications to cure the common cold haven't been discovered yet, scientists and researchers have developed medications that treat mental illnesses, reduce pain after surgery, and lower cholesterol, just to name a few. Medications can destroy cancer cells, stop allergic reactions, kill the AIDS virus, and protect our bodies against measles, mumps, and chicken pox.

Highly specialized treatments and surgeries continue to save lives. Blocked arteries in a person's heart are stinted, which creates healthy blood flow. Cancerous tumors are removed, and life is restored. Weight is lost and health is regained when a stomach is stapled to allow in only the necessary amount of food.

Imagine a world without these instruments of healing. My life would be dramatically different. I may not even be alive. How about you?

Record healing(s) you have experienced because of man-made medications and treatments.

MASKING THE TRUE SYMPTOMS

Over the decades of her illness, Tiffany [L] has experienced the benefits and the shortfalls of man-made medications. Her journey started during one of her high school cheerleading practices. She felt tingling in her hands and feet, combined with a lack of endurance. Because Tiffany had no reason to know those symptoms were warning signs of an invisible illness, she ignored them.

During her first pregnancy, her obstetrician became concerned with her extreme vomiting, dehydration, and fainting. The severity of her symptoms led to several overnight hospital stays. During one of those hospital stays, a neurologist stopped by to chat with her. He felt her pregnancy might be masking the true symptoms of an invisible illness. He ordered an electroencephalogram (EEG) and an electrocardiogram (EKG). After studying the results, the neurologist said, "Your results are fine, but I believe you have multiple sclerosis (MS)."

She heard what he said, but she thought, "You're a quack. You've only done a few tests." However, the tingling in her head, neck, and feet was impossible to ignore. A few months after giving birth to her son, her vision changed drastically.

The additional symptoms concerned her, so Tiffany scheduled an appointment with an ophthalmologist. He diagnosed her with optic neuritis—damage to the optic nerve from inflammation—and insisted she see a neurologist, who instructed her to have a magnetic resonance imaging (MRI). "Combined with your previous EEG and EKG results, your MRI confirms a diagnosis of multiple sclerosis (MS). There are six plaques on your brain," the neurologist explained.

At just twenty-seven years of age, Tiffany struggled to process the news that she had a progressive neurological disease. A disease that would slowly attack her brain and spinal cord. She felt broken and wondered if she'd be in a wheelchair for the rest of her life. *Would she slowly go blind? Would she suddenly become paralyzed?*

These fears threatened to defeat her at the onset of her journey. Her enemy, MS, might be a difficult adversary, but Tiffany knew the enemy's weakness is God. She spoke aloud her trust and reliance in God by repeating 2 Samuel 22:33 many times, which says, "It is God who arms me with strength and keeps my way secure."

ABSOLUTELY NO CONTROL

Tiffany described her journey with MS as a roller coaster ride of twists and turns and always having to wrestle with her 'MS monster.' Her weekly treatments slow the progression, but she still experiences pain, unrelenting fatigue, brain fog, and periods of anxiety and depression.

Knowing these symptoms are chronic could defeat her. Tiffany admitted, "Honestly, it does every so often." Her motto on those tough days/weeks/months is "Happiness is a choice." She can choose to focus on those symptoms and feel unhappy. Or she can choose to focus on the blessings all around her and feel happy, which is exactly what she chooses. Early on in her journey, Tiffany decided to maintain a 'challenges won't stop me' mindset.

When flare-ups hit every eighteen months or so, Tiffany is reminded MS is a progressive disease. Her symptoms will increase over time. Her positive attitude about life and her joy are the same regardless of when she will experience complete healing. Instead of feeling defeated by a lack of healing, she is grateful for the slow progression of symptoms over the last twenty-five years. Tiffany believes the slow progression is the result of her prayers and the prayers of many others.

Tiffany decided long ago to trust that God is walking this challenging health journey with her. She said, "I know I have absolutely no control over this disease. All I go through would tear me down if I didn't lean on the Lord. God brings peace when my fear is high. Knowing He is in control takes the pressure off me to try and figure it all out. I know

God sees the full picture of my life. If I rely on Him, and not on what I think might happen in the future, I have joy, peace, and happiness."

A few years ago, Tiffany was diagnosed with osteoporosis, a bone disease that is caused by a decrease in bone density and bone mass. Additionally, her MS is progressing. These unexpected turns interrupted her path, but she is determined to keep fighting. Osteoporosis and her MS progressing might be the hotter flames of a refining fire. Nevertheless, Tiffany believes the additional dross being scraped away will result in God seeing His image in her.

Tiffany regularly lifts her binoculars above her struggles, so that she can focus on God more clearly. Her map is well-worn, as is her multi-purpose tool. Companions draw near, offering their encouragement and support. Tiffany's connection to God strengthens her and fills her with the courage to keep moving forward.

Reread or skim Tiffany's story. Highlight her responses to challenges, snakes, and refining fires.

JESUS' FORGIVENESS

What if the healing you are desperate for is not physical, mental, financial, emotional, or relational? Friends and family have shared their belief that your actions, choices, and habits are destroying your life. And your health. You're finally ready to admit that the root cause of your challenges is sin. As such, your sins are negatively impacting your physical health, your mental health, your finances, and your relationships. Jesus forgiving your sins is the healing you need. May Jesus' responses in the following Bible stories encourage you to turn away from your sin and turn to Jesus.

In Luke 7, a woman who lived a sinful life came to a Pharisee's house where Jesus was eating. The Pharisee didn't offer any of a host's expected hospitality to Jesus. However, the woman with a sinful past offered hospitality to Jesus by wetting His feet with her tears, kissing His feet, and then pouring perfume on His feet. Despite being a sinner, Jesus turned to her and said, "Your sins are forgiven ... Your faith has saved you; go in peace" (Luke 7:47, 50). The sinful woman sought the only One who could heal her pain, the broken relationships, and the misery her sinful life had caused: Jesus. We aren't privy to the rest of her story, but I believe Jesus forgiving her sins completely changed her life.

RESTORED TO PERFECT HEALTH

Many lessons can be gleaned from the story of the man at the pool of Bethesda who had been an invalid for thirty-eight years. In this powerful story, Jesus saw him and asked, "Do you want to get well?" (John 5:6). What a strange question, right? Strange yes, but there's more happening than meets the eye.

Commentary on the Gospel of St. John by St. Thomas Aquinas provides explanations and interpretations to help us understand this story. In lecture 1, Aquinas explained, "God gave to that water [at the pool of Bethesda] the power to heal so that men by washing might learn through their bodily health to seek their spiritual health.[2] The man who could not be cured by the pool was to be cured by Christ, because those whom the law could not heal, Christ heals perfectly.[3] Jesus saw him [the invalid man] not only with his physical eyes, but also with the eyes of his mercy ... He [Jesus] did not say this because he did not know the answer, for it was quite evident that the man wanted to be healed, he said it to arouse the sick man's desire, and to show his patience in waiting so many years to be cured of his sickness and in not giving up." [4]

Describe what you think Aquinas meant by "might learn through their bodily health to seek spiritual health."

Aquinas continued, "The Lord commanded both the nature of the man and his will, for both are under the Lord's power. He commanded his nature when he said, Stand up. This command was not directed to the man's will, for this was not within the power of his will. But it was within the power of his nature, to which the Lord gave the power to stand by his command. He gave two commands to the man's will: pick up your mat and walk! The literal meaning for this is that these two things were commanded in order to show that the man had been restored to perfect health. For in all his miracles the Lord produced a perfect work." [5]

The invalid man was healed, but his interaction with Jesus wasn't finished. "Later Jesus found him at the temple and said to him, 'See you are well again. Stop sinning or something worse will happen'" (John 5:14). Jesus reminded the paralytic man of his physical healing. And He told the man what would happen if he didn't stop sinning.

While the invalid's physical healing was important, Jesus was more concerned about the man's spiritual healing. A person's spiritual healing holds far greater importance. The apostle Paul explained why our spiritual healing holds far greater importance in Romans 6:22-23, which says, "But now that you've found you don't have to listen to sin tell you what to do, and have discovered the delight of listening to God telling you, what a surprise! A whole, healed, put-together life right now, with more and more of life on the way! Work hard for sin your whole life and your pension is death. But God's gift is real life, eternal life, delivered by Jesus, our Master" (MSG).

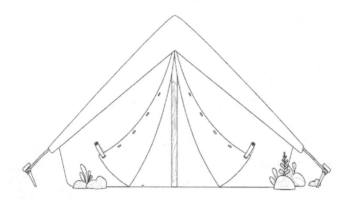

HUMBLY BOW AT HIS FEET

Do either of these Bible stories resonate with you? Would your actions and choices be labeled sinful by others, like the woman in Luke 7? If so, notice how she cried many tears at Jesus' feet, kissing them, and pouring perfume on them. Her brokenness over her sinful life led her to Jesus' feet. You, too, can humbly bow at His feet and ask Him to forgive you of your sins. He will forgive you. And you will receive spiritual healing just as the woman in Luke 7 did.

Are physical challenges hiding your sins like the man in John 5? We can only see your visible challenges, but Jesus sees your heart and the sin that is the root cause of your challenges. In His kindness, He may grant you physical healing. But He wants more for you, and so do I. You can also experience the healing of your soul when you repent of you sins and accept His forgiveness.

If you continue to cling tightly to your sins, your sins will continue to separate you from God. But they don't have to. Jesus died on the cross and was resurrected from the dead so that you can be forgiven of your sins. I know it may be hard to humble yourself and repent of your sins. Oftentimes, the hardest things in life lead to the best outcomes. I promise Jesus washing away your sins and receiving His forgiveness is a thousand times better than any outcome you could imagine.

If you've turned away from your sin and accepted Jesus for the first time, or you're recommitting your life to Him, feel free to email me at reader7writer@gmail.com. I would love to rejoice with you!

IT WASN'T THAT EASY

Pain invaded Dianne's  life at a young age. "I'm doing this because I love you so much," were the horrific words Dianne's father said numerous times throughout the years he sexually abused her. Tranquilizers used to numb her migraine pain also became a way for her to escape her deep emotional pain.

When she was sixteen, Dianne threatened to kill her father if he ever touched her again. His abusive behavior stopped, but her healing wouldn't come for many, many years. An invitation to turn tricks provided the money she needed for the drugs already controlling her. "I liked the idea of prostitution as it would allow me to be in control of men. I thought it would be a way to 'stick it' to my abusive father, knowing he'd be mortified," Dianne shared.

Thinking prostitution wasn't a big deal, she convinced herself she could detach from the sexual act. "Once I started, I realized it wasn't that easy. Emotionally, I felt sick, even nauseous. It was degrading to have a man paw at me. I thought I was in control, but I really had no control at all," Dianne shared. A pimp introduced her to heroin and Dilaudid. "When I did those drugs, I didn't feel anything or care about anything. I just wanted to die. I even tried to overdose twice and failed both times."

A fractured relationship with her mother, who was emotionally distant throughout her childhood, combined with an abusive father, caused Dianne to have a warped understanding of love. When she left home at seventeen, she found love in a female friend. However, relationships with men and women didn't fill the empty cavern inside of her. Neither did drugs. Two years in detox centers revealed additional struggles: a porn addiction, bipolar disorder, suicidal behaviors, and an eating disorder. "Once they figured out I had mental problems, the doctors moved me to a mental ward," she shared. Dianne described the next eighteen years of being in and out of mental institutions as a roller coaster ride. Self-hatred and feelings of worthlessness drove her into darkness.

Dianne visited church with a friend during those years, but she never felt comfortable as she knew her life choices didn't align with God's Word. But Jesus kept tugging at Dianne's heart. One early Sunday morning, Dianne hit rock bottom when the woman she was living with packed her bags and walked out the door. Dianne recalled, "My life was falling apart. I desperately wanted to commit suicide. I cried out to God that I couldn't live this way anymore. I didn't want this life of pain. I begged for Him to take me. Even though I wanted to kill myself, I was afraid it was a sin, and I'd go to hell."

BELIEVED SO MANY LIES

While sitting in her living room alone, Dianne had a vision: "I saw myself as God sees me. I felt His overwhelming love. I felt him say I was beautiful— that I wasn't a drug addict. That I wasn't a lesbian. I couldn't stop crying. I realized I was not who I thought I was. All my life, I'd believed so many lies. It was liberating to see how God sees me and to experience His love. I was so grateful He never gave up on me."

God lifted her above the lies of the enemy. On Dianne's rock bottom day, she experienced Psalm 147:3, which says, "He heals the brokenhearted and binds up their wounds." Committing her life to Jesus was a significant turning point in her journey.

Psalm 103:1-5 is Dianne's continuous praise for the freedom she's found in Jesus. These verses proclaim: "O my soul, bless GOD. From head to toe, I'll bless his holy name! O my soul, bless GOD, don't forget a single blessing! He forgives your sins—every one. He heals your diseases—every one. He redeems you from hell—saves your life! He crowns you with love and mercy—a paradise crown. He wraps you in goodness—beauty eternal. He renews your youth—you're always young in his presence" (MSG).

Forgiving her father released the shame and anger that consumed her. Forgiveness and restoration healed the relationship with her mother, even to the point that Dianne's mother lived with her until her passing. Numbing her mind and body with drugs and alcohol was replaced with an insatiable hunger for God's Word and prayer. Understanding her identity in Christ wiped out all confusion about her sexual identity. Her spiritual healing is nothing short of miraculous. During her interview, Dianne proclaimed, "I was fully healed the day I accepted Jesus into my heart. He, and He alone, took away the pain, shame, sexual orientation confusion, mental illness struggles, and desire for drugs and alcohol."

The good God meant for Dianne looks like loving, laughing, caring for one another, and growing in Christ over the last twenty-five years with her husband, Mike. Many of Dianne's years have been painful, but she's the first to admit that all she learned during those years is invaluable. Serving others who are hurting is Dianne's passion. Through Victoria's Friends, an Atlanta-based non-profit, Diane shares God's message of love, forgiveness, and healing with women who are lost and trapped in the helplessness of working in sexually oriented businesses. Additionally, Dianne teaches and mentors women at her church.

NOT BEING HEALED

We must address 'the elephant blocking the trail.' Man-made medications and treatments do not cure or heal every physical, mental, or emotional condition. They are limited. This reality can anger every one of us, especially those with mental or chronic illnesses. It often angers those who fell into a deep sadness after a loved one was treated with medications, fought hard, and still passed away. Often, we question God, blaming Him for not healing us or a loved one when we know it is within His power to do so.

While complete healing is within His power, we aren't omniscient —having infinite awareness, understanding, and insight—like God. Isaiah 55:8-9 explains it best: "I [God] don't think the way you think. The way you work isn't the way I work.' GOD's Decree. 'For as the sky soars high above earth, so the way I work surpasses the way you work, and the way I think is beyond the way you think'" (MSG). His infinite awareness, understanding, and insight far exceed our limited aware- ness, understanding, and insight. Therefore, we must trust the timing of His healing.

One evening recently, I couldn't stop thinking about a close friend who passed away after her second battle with ovarian cancer. Just a year before her passing, D's husband dropped her off at a chemo appointment, drove home, laid down for a nap, and never woke up. His unexpected passing was devastating. As much as she wanted to get lost in her grief, her ovarian cancer  demanded her attention. Through her tears, D kept fighting hard. She passed away a year after her husband. Her son and daughter spoke at her memorial service, sharing what we all knew about D: joy and love flowed through her like a rushing river, impacting every single person she met.

NECESSARY FOR YOUR GROWTH

As I drove home from D's memorial service, I asked God, "Why did You heal D's cancer the first time but not this time?" Several minutes of silence passed. Then, I recalled a conference I attended many years ago. The speaker walked across the stage and held up the backside of a finished cross-stitch piece. By all accounts, the back side was a disaster. She asked if we would prominently display this side of the artwork in our home. A collective 'No' rumbled through the auditorium.

The speaker paused, giving the audience a few moments to think. Then, she said words I'll never forget: "It may look as if the cross stitcher didn't follow the pattern. Notice how some threads haphazardly intersect or overlap other threads. See the numerous knots?" She grabbed a dangling thread. "What's going on here? To an onlooker, this is a mess. But suppose I told you the cross-stitcher was God. Would you think differently about the appearance of the backside?"

She continued, "God knows that which looks like a mess is actually a masterpiece. The backside represents His workings in your life. Ever heard the expression, 'God's thoughts surpass our thoughts? His ways surpass our ways?' Well, this backside is a perfect example. You might not have chosen to stitch the details of your life in this seemingly haphazard way, but God's stitches (or His ways) are accomplishing His intended purpose for your life. Take these dangling threads; they must be snipped. Just like the pruning described in John 15. We won't always understand the reason for the specific stitches God chose because His ways are not our ways."

Images of past situations and relationships popped up in my mind. I agreed that the back side of my life might look like a mess to some. But before I had a chance to wonder what the front side of my life might look like, the presenter flipped the cross-stitched piece over, revealing the front side. "Gorgeous, isn't it? When your life comes to an end, and God invites you to see yourself in your completed form, you'll understand why He stitched situations, challenges, and relationships in knotted threads here, crisscrossed threads there, and snipped any dangling threads. All those threads were necessary for your growth. Oh, I didn't ignore that frayed thread. It's the thread that needed healing. God didn't ignore your prayers for healing. You did receive healing. Just not like you pictured it."

All throughout your life, God healed your dead ends and failures by knotting them, so you wouldn't keep trying to make them work. Your doctor suggested a treatment for your health condition. You experienced minimal improvement, which increased your frustration. Then another doctor prescribed medication, which only relieved some of the symptoms. Increasing the number of times you exercised each week strengthened your body. Lastly, you combined the treatment, the medication, and exercise with acupuncture. After a few weeks, you realized your symptoms hadn't completely disappeared but were manageable. Your healing came in the intersecting or overlapping of those threads.

Maybe you realized a close friend was no longer putting in any effort, but you couldn't imagine ending the friendship. Because God knew that friendship was a festering wound, He healed your heart by snipping or pruning that relationship. In His infinite awareness, understanding, and insight, God sees the backside *and* the front-side of your life simultaneously, knowing each thread serves a specific purpose in you becoming a masterpiece!"

The audience's response? Stunned silence.

Take a few minutes to think about what your life might look like on the backside of a cross-stitched piece. While your front-side masterpiece is still in process, can you imagine His purpose for the knots? For the frayed threads? For the snipped threads? For the intersected threads? If so, describe them below.

How does knowing His thoughts and His ways are above yours help you accept your partial healing?

UNLIKE ANY OTHER

Actress Sophia Bush offers wisdom that reiterates this concept: "You are allowed to be both a masterpiece and a work in progress, simultaneously." [6] When you truly believe Jesus is creating a masterpiece in you, it's easier to trust the crazy backside of your life as a work in progress. Remember fighting to overcome isn't just about surviving challenges. It's also about thriving. May I challenge you to thrive—to grow vigorously; flourish; and make progress toward your goals despite or because of circumstances—while your healing is in progress?

Your first aid kit is unlike any other first aid kit. Man-made medications and treatments may heal your illnesses and injuries. But I believe Jesus is where true healing is found. Jesus is the salve your body, mind, and soul longs for. Though you might not always see it or understand it, His way of treating and healing your illnesses and injuries is the healing that is creating you into a masterpiece. Pack your first aid kit, so we can journey on!

> Don't be surprised by pain. Be surprised by joy, be surprised by the little flower that shows its
>
> beauty in the midst of a barren desert and be surprised by the immense healing power that keeps
>
> bursting forth like springs of fresh water from the depth of our pain. 7
>
> —Theologian Henri Nouwen

mile 15

Have You Noticed the Gifts Scattered Throughout the Difficult Parts of Your Journey?

What seems to us bitter trials are often blessings in disguise.1

—Irish poet and playwright, Oscar Wilde

During the first mile of *Keep Moving Forward*, we fortified our trust in and reliance on Jesus by remaining connected to Him. A mile of growing and thriving despite the numerous challenges of life followed. Then, we endured a mile of fiery and painful refining fires. Despite being weary, I'm so grateful you kept moving forward with me to the next mile because our companions joined us! Only to be followed by a lengthy mile of our fears and enemies hissing at us. And the last mile reminded us Jesus is our healing salve for every illness and injury.

You may be wondering, "Where are you taking us now?" A good place. I promise. Though I must tell you the uphill hike will be challenging. Don't trip on the roots. Around the half-mile point, step over the mud hole where the baby snakes live. Don't forget to hydrate along the way. When you get to the bench near the sharp right turn, stop for a rest. Just don't settle there. Keep moving forward! What's the good place at the end of the mile? A majestic waterfall!

Anticipate the surge of refreshment you'll feel when you stand near the powerful cascade of water. Expect a deeply felt peace to wash over you. The water flowing over the crest, bouncing across the rocks, and rushing to the pool at the base is hypnotizing. The stress and worry your challenge is causing you will slowly fade. I'm tempted to run straight there. But the gifts scattered along this difficult mile are too good to miss. I'm excited to show you!

Author Christine Kloser believes, "Every challenge is a gift waiting to be unwrapped." [2] The words 'challenge' and 'gift' in the same sentence seem like an oxymoron. Can those really coexist? Yes, I'll show you how.

In the previous paragraph, please highlight, "Every challenge is a gift waiting to be unwrapped."

Read both of the following prompts first. Then answer the prompt that best describes your feelings.

Describe why knowing your challenge is a gift doesn't change how you feel about your challenge. Describe how knowing your challenge is a gift changes how you feel about your challenge and encourages you to unwrap it.

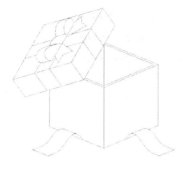 No matter how much you want to take the waterfall at the end of this mile home with you, such majesty and beauty can't possibly fit in your back-pack. So, the visual image of a gift box will represent the blessings or gifts scattered along the difficult weeks/months/years of your challenge. Seek to unwrap every gift God scatters along the difficult parts of your journey.

PART OF GOD'S DESIGN

The challenges we face in life, as painful and difficult as they may be, are part of God's design. So are His blessings. James, Jesus' brother, described this dichotomy: "Blessed (happy, to be envied) is the man who is patient under trial and stands up under temptation, for when he has stood the test and been approved, he will receive [the victor's] crown of life which God has promised to those who love Him" (James 1:12, AMPC).

In literature, this verse would be called an if-then conditional statement. You might know it as cause and effect. A recent *Psychology Today* article sheds light on why 'if-then conditional statements' are powerful motivators. Dr. Halvorson explained, "Amazingly, you are two to three times more likely to succeed if you use an if-then plan than if you don't." [3]

Highlight the two difficult challenges or 'if statements' in James 1:12.

Choose a different color highlighter. Now, highlight the two blessings or 'then statements.'

Describe how knowing you will be approved and will receive the victor's crown of life (two blessings) does or does not motivate you to be patient under trial and stand up under temptation (two difficult challenges).

James' words are meant to encourage you. When you are patient under trial and when you stand up under temptation, God notices. Remain faithful to Him when the trials, temptations, and tests of life strive to defeat you, destroy you, or wear you down to the point of wanting to give up. When you couldn't imagine your circumstances getting better, God noticed your decision to trust Him. He noticed how you stood strong when the enemy tried to weaken you. Being blessed and the victor's crown are God's generous gifts to you. Blessings during your earthly life. And blessings in heaven. You'll receive the victor's crown of life!

STRENGTH ON A WARRIOR

King David faced many trials, temptations, and tests. Was he patient under trial? Did he stand up under temptation? Sometimes, yes. Sometimes, no.

While David was not perfect, God promised, "I have bestowed strength on a warrior; I have raised up a young man from among the people. I have found David my servant; with my sacred oil I have anointed him. My hand will sustain him; surely my arm will strengthen him. The enemy will not get the better of him; the wicked will not oppress him. I will crush his foes before him and strike down his adversaries. My faithful love will be with him, and through my name his horn will be exalted." (Psalm 89:19-24).

Write your name above 'young man,' 'David,' and every instance of 'him' or 'his' in Psalm 89:19-24.

Now, with your name inserted, reread these verses aloud. Describe how reading your name in these verses impacts you.

Go back through Psalms 89:19-24 and highlight each of the statements describing what God did and promised to do for David.

Just as God promised to do these for David, God promises to do them for you. These promises are His gifts to you. Gifts scattered along the difficult parts of your path. What are those promises and gifts? God strengthens you, anoints you, sustains you, and doesn't allow the enemy to get the better of you or oppress you. God crushes your foes and strikes down your adversaries. God's faithful love is with you. And through His name, you will be exalted. May these gifts motivate you to stand strong, fight to overcome, and keep moving forward!

FLOWING WITHIN

My friend, Karen, doesn't just teach middle school science. She is passionate about her students understanding a Creator named God designed every detail of our world. Our God created significance and purpose in every detail of every created thing in nature. A beautiful and majestic waterfall is no exception. As gorgeous as a waterfall's outer appearance is, all that is flowing within its waters are the true gifts.

A river flowing into the crest, or top, of a waterfall carries sediment from many miles upstream. *Sediment*, or microscopic silt, pebbles, and rocks, flowing within the water, are irritants. The root word *irritate* means "to provoke impatience, anger, or displeasure in; annoy."

Have any of your challenges caused impatience, anger, displeasure in, or annoyance? Yeah, some of mine have too. The word provoke in the definition of *irritate* stood out like the sole jersey-clad Pirates fan at a Braves game. *Provoke* means "to call forth a feeling or action; to stir up purposely; to provide the needed stimulus for; to incite."

Sediment are irritants that provoke or provide needed stimulus. Stimulus for what? Sediment stimulates, or actively stirs up, the water, creating a waterfall's melody. Besides a waterfall's outward beauty, its melody—or the sweet, agreeable arrangement of sounds—captivates those who draw near it.

Music is my husband Jeff's love language. During the day, he's a mortgage loan officer. After work, he metaphorically steps into a phone booth like Clark Kent. Instead of donning a Superman cape with the intention of fighting for truth, justice, and the American way, he throws on his favorite '80s T-shirt and grabs his purple Jackson guitar. Jeff often warms up by playing melodies. Among them are melodies by Latin jazz musician, Carlos Santana.

Santana believes, "There's a melody in everything. And once you find the melody, then you connect immediately with the heart ... But nothing penetrates the heart faster than the melody." [4] If Santa is correct in asserting a melody is in everything, then please allow me to replace the word 'everything' with 'challenges.' Let's look at the revised statement: There is a melody in challenges. Hmmm ... what say you?

Describe why you agree or disagree with 'There is a melody in your challenges.'

HOW WE RESPOND TO THE SEDIMENT

I spent some time thinking about Santana's words. A waterfall isn't given a choice about its response to the sediment/irritants. Its involuntary response to the sediment stirring within its waters is the melody. We, on the other hand, do have a choice about how we respond to the sediment, or challenges, in our lives.

Suppose a challenge stirs up a constant flow of bitterness and resentment in you. You respond by choosing angry words and complaining about your circumstances. These not-so-pleasing sounds will not create a melody. On the other hand, suppose your challenge stirs up grit, determination, and a 'challenges won't stop me' mindset. You respond by choosing laughter when things go awry while boldly declaring your trust in God. These pleasing sounds will create a melody —a sweet, agreeable arrangement of sounds. A melody in your heart and your life. A beautiful melody for all to experience.

How are you responding to the sediment, or challenges, in your life?

Describe how your response is or is not creating a melody.

IMPEDING THE PATH

Years ago, a teenaged girl named Mila looked forward to meeting up with her dad at noon at the base of the waterfall downstream. With the way things were going, there wouldn't be any trout to show her dad. Frustrated with the lack of bites on her line, Mila considered her gear and the environment.

Her dad, a skilled fisherman, recommended the artificial flies as bait, so they couldn't be the reason. She'd found a deep hole with a slow current, so her location couldn't be the reason. While planning the trip, her dad shared, "Early morning or late in the evening are the best times to catch trout." She'd waded to this spot in the river half an hour before the rooster even thought about crowing, so her timing couldn't be the reason. "Why am I not catching any fish?" Mila shouted.

When Mila crouched down, she noticed all the rocks impeding the path to her bait. She scooped up a handful of water. When the water drained away, twigs and pebbly sand remained in her hand. "Ah! The large rocks and sediment are preventing fish from reaching my bait. If I remove all the rocks and sediment, surely, I will catch a basket full of trout."

The late morning sun beat down on Mila as she moved large rocks to the riverbank. Removing all the sediment proved to be an exceptionally arduous task. Exhausted but hopeful after two hours of work, she finally cast her line. Mila's earlier frustrations paled in comparison to the anger and annoyance she felt when she realized the fish were still not biting.

At eleven-thirty, Mila climbed out of the river and grabbed her gear. As she walked to the base of the waterfall to meet her dad, she grumbled about the futility of removing the rocks and sediment. Thirty minutes later, Mila realized she was lost. She remembered her dad saying, "You're directly upstream from the waterfall. When it's time to meet me, follow the sound of the waterfall." Unfortunately, she didn't hear any rushing water.

Mila pulled out her map. As luck would have it, she'd wandered near a stream labeled on her map. She located the base of the waterfall on the map, course-corrected, and began hiking. Mila hiked back to the river and then toward the waterfall. She realized she could barely hear what should have been rushing water. As she walked toward the waterfall, Mila noticed a confused look on her dad's face.

A FISH TALE

Mila dropped her rod and basket by a tree and stood next to her dad. He continued studying the waterfall. He glanced at Mila and said, "I'm just wondering what happened to this waterfall's melody. Its roar is missing. Instead of the beautiful volume and  intensity of other waterfalls we've seen, this one is meek and flowing slowly. Such a strange sight."

It suddenly occurred to Mila that the sediment she'd removed from the river upstream had profoundly impacted this waterfall. "Why is your face so red?" her dad asked. She looked toward the waterfall and said, "I've got a fish tale you'll never believe, Dad."

You know Mila's fish tale isn't a true story. No one would try to remove the sediment/irritants/challenges from their life, would they? If given the opportunity, I believe most of us would. But just like with Mila's efforts, it's futile. The sediment/irritants/challenges flowing within our lives are necessary. Remember mile 02 in *Challenges Won't Stop Me?* Just as Santana said, "There's a melody in everything." Including challenges. Let's choose to allow the challenges in our lives to create a beautiful melody in us.

Not until I researched waterfalls had I thought about all that's happening within a waterfall. Understanding the purpose of sediment flowing within one makes me appreciate Rishabh Gautam's words: "Waterfalls wouldn't sound so melodious if there were no rocks in their way." [5]

Return to the sections titled FLOWING WITHIN and HOW WE RESPOND TO THE SEDIMENT. Highlight the gifts found within the waterfall as you skim those sections.

Now, write each of those gifts around the gift box.

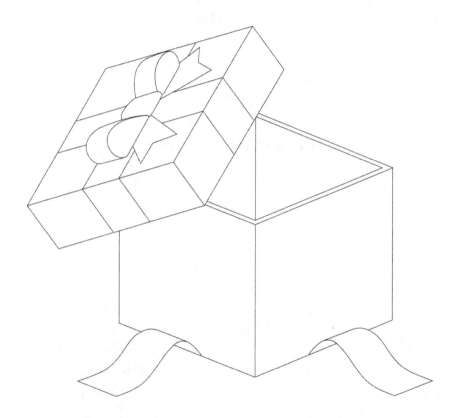

MET HER PRINCE CHARMING

As you read Tamiko's story, underline the pieces of sediment (challenges) flowing within her life. Highlight the waterfalls (gifts).

Tamiko [N] grew up in a poverty-stricken neighborhood to drug-addicted parents. Even though she worked hard to hide their destructive habits, everyone knew. Kids teased her about her family situation. While in high school, she dated an athlete who was from a wealthy family. For a while she was OK with his attention and gifts, but he began forcing her to do things she didn't want to do. Not until many years later did she realize the way he would squeeze her hand tightly and how he spoke to her, including threatening her, were controlling and abusive behaviors.

In her twenties, Tamiko met a man who owned a Fortune 500 company. Victor (a pseudonym to protect his identity) promised, "I feel I was put on this earth to take care of you. When we get married, you won't have to work, and you can be a stay-at-home mom." She believed she'd met her prince charming. A year of dating led to Victor and Tamiko getting married. "Things changed very quickly. He became very controlling," she shared. He kept his promises about Tamiko not having to work and staying home to take care of their kids. But not working put her at a serious disadvantage. She didn't have her own money. Victor gave her an allowance to buy groceries and clothing, but when she needed anything else, Tamiko had to ask him for money.

Victor's faith was one of the traits that drew her in when they were dating. But as a husband, he used Scriptures to control her. Insisting she needed to be more submissive lined up with his need to control her. He refused to go to church with her and believed she spent too much time there. Keeping Tamiko from her faith—the place where she drew her strength—broke her. His relentless emotional, financial, verbal, and spiritual abuse wrecked her confidence and self-esteem. Studying God's Word strengthened Tamiko.

Victor's controlling and abusive behaviors became progressively worse. He began pushing and shoving her; she felt like she deserved it. "I was always scrambling to figure out what I could do better to make him love me more. That's all I wanted."

Five years into their marriage, everything changed. While Tamiko and Victor were driving on the interstate, she told him she was leaving him. He replied, "If you leave, I will kill both of us." Victor grabbed the steering wheel from her, causing the car to spin a few times. After the car stopped spinning, he beat her and strangled her until she was unconscious.

When Tamiko came to, a woman approached her and said, "My husband and I saw everything. The police are on the way." Seeing Victor arrested became Tamiko's turning point. "I began putting things in place to start my life over. I moved into a one-bedroom apartment with my children. Sleeping on an air mattress that first night provided the most peace we'd experienced in five years," she explained.

I'M STILL STANDING

Several years later, Tamiko spent time reflecting on her past relationships. She concluded that her relationships were "same guy, different face." Each man looked different, but all were controlling, possessive, and abusive. She spent time connecting with God. In the silence, she heard His voice revealing the purpose for her pain.

Her book, *Wounds to Wisdom: I'm Still Standing,* is a testimony of her challenges creating melodies.

God gifted Tamiko with a passion to prevent others from experiencing the pain of domestic violence. She formed a non-profit called The Still Standing Alliance, which focuses on domestic violence advocacy, awareness, and prevention. Tamiko's ministry is evidence of the beauty that blooms after pounding rain. Her tagline is "Turning pain into purpose." She believes, "The adversities, trials, and tribulations we experience are preparing us. We don't know it while we are in it, but God is preparing us for something greater and pushing us into our purpose."

In addition to her podcast, Living the Empowered Life, Tamiko ministers to women who have overcome life's adversities. In her Living the Empowered Life masterclass, she coaches clients to turn their painful experiences into transformational businesses. Tamiko works hard, so she can enjoy life to the fullest. She and her husband, Kenny, enjoy digging into a bowl full of Lays BBQ kettle chips while binge-watching the latest shows on Netflix.

HIDDEN BEHIND

A waterfall's gifts aren't limited to those flowing within it. Equally valuable are the gifts hidden behind a waterfall. For various reasons, not all parks grant access to the rock shelter, or cave, that is hidden behind a waterfall. Our metaphorical waterfall is safe, so we've been granted access behind it. Follow me!

The rock shelter—or the space hidden behind a waterfall—offers safety, protection, and refuge. A waterfall is a gorgeous oasis in the middle of a forest. Why would you need safety, protection, or refuge?

Severe weather conditions and/or wild animals are challenges you might encounter while walking in the forest. Severe weather-type challenges and/or wild animal-type challenges have likely impacted your life. Don't believe me?

How about juggling the heavy downpour of doctor's appointments during your unexpected health crisis? Remember when anxiety attacks clapped like thunder, one after another? How about your friend's unkind words striking hot like lightning? Remember the unsolicited judgments about your parenting decisions pelting you like icy hail? How about when those gale force winds of your layoff knocked you down?

Perhaps your challenges don't mimic fierce weather conditions. Maybe, your marriage is as rabid as a raccoon bite. How about the growling bear named work responsibilities that stands between you and time with your family? You already know about the poisonous snake bites of your fears and enemies. Whichever severe weather-like or wild animal-like challenge intersects your path, you will need a safe shelter to hide in.

GOD'S GIFT OF FAITHFULNESS

Those who venture behind a waterfall to explore or seek safety in the rock shelter will discover a hidden treasure: a rainbow. Look through the cascading water and you'll see a gorgeous spectrum of colors. Maybe like me, a rainbow reminds you of Noah.

Noah was described as a righteous man, blameless among the people of his time. He walked faithfully with God. In contrast, God saw how corrupt the earth and the people had become. Intending to destroy the earth by flood, God instructed Noah to build an ark (Genesis 6:5-23). Details are not given about all the ways God provided for Noah and his family during the hundred and fifty days of the flood, but you can bet He did. No amount of Dramamine could have warded off seasickness. God's gift.

Where did their food and the animals' food come from? Noah and his family didn't feast on the creatures within the ark. Genesis 8:19 says, "All the animals and all the creatures that move along the ground and all the birds—everything that moves on land—came out of the ark, one kind after another." Because *all* the animals, creatures, and birds came out of the ark, it would seem God gifted them food.

When the flood waters dried, Noah built an altar and sacrificed a burnt offering. The ark offered refuge from God's wrath. Noah knew God sparing his life, as well as the lives of his family, were gifts. Imagine the gratitude he felt when he realized all the ways God protected his family and kept them safe.

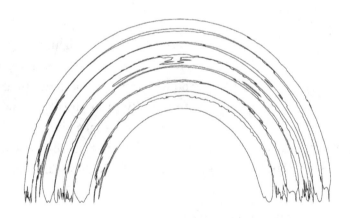

Then God established a covenant with Noah, his sons, and every living creature on earth: "Never again will all life be destroyed by the waters of a flood; never again will there be a flood to destroy the earth" (Genesis 9:14). To seal the covenant, God explained, "I have set my rainbow in the clouds, and it will be the sign of the covenant between me and the earth. Whenever I bring clouds over the earth and the rainbow appears in the clouds, I will remember my covenant between me and you and all living creatures of every kind. Never again will the waters become a flood to destroy all life" (Genesis 9:13-15).

The rainbow is God's gift of faithfulness to His children. Even though we can trust that God is faithful during our struggles, you likely won't see the gift of the rainbow until after your challenge. When you reflect on the challenges you've faced, fingerprints of His faithfulness will be scattered all along your difficult path.

Psalm 25:10 lists three gifts that accompany God's faithfulness. This verse says, "All the paths of the Lord are mercy and steadfast love, even truth and faithfulness are they for those who keep His covenant and His testimonies" (AMPC).

Highlight the three gifts that accompany God's faithfulness.

SPRINGING UP BENEATH THE RAIN

Before we leave this hidden shelter, I invite you to notice the view. At some of the smaller waterfalls, the width of the rushing water obstructs your view. Perhaps your challenge is obstructing your view. While you might not readily agree, obstructions can also be gifts. Humans are a curious bunch. We want to know and understand everything happening in our lives. Sometimes, we just don't need to know. In those cases, an obstructed view is a gift.

Often, the cascading water doesn't completely obstruct your view. Scooch to the left or right and behold the expansive view. Would you agree the mountains look grander, the trees taller, and the sun brighter?

The perspective from this hiding place invites you to observe the whole forest, and not just the trees. You can see how the forest is interconnected. Each part contributes to the whole. Each part of the forest needs the other parts to survive. This interconnectedness creates breathtaking scenery and a thriving ecosystem.

From this perspective, you can see tiny trees and plants growing in what were once burned areas of the forest. You surmise that fire is necessary for new growth. An upended tree with a shallow root system reminds you how harshly an unrelenting, heavy rain can impact you. Change your view, and it changes your perspective. Savor the gift of perspective.

The numerous gifts flowing within and those hidden behind the waterfall prepare you and equip you for everything God has in store for you. In the June 15th devotion of *Streams in the Desert*, J.M.M. shares this wisdom: "If you will only believe your Dad's Word, you will realize that springing up beneath the pounding rain are spiritual flowers. And they are more beautiful and fragrant than those that ever grew before in your stormless and suffering-free life." [6]

I love how J.M.M. describes us as "spiritual flowers." Did you notice the 'if-then' statement? Spiritual flowers spring up *after* the pounding rain! I bet there are rainbows in the sky, too.

MARKED BY AN INABILITY TO READ

As you read Cathie's story, highlight her challenges. Draw flowers beside the gifts God scattered throughout the difficult parts of her journey.

When I look at my best friend, Cathie's [O], life, I see miles upon miles of the spiritual flowers J.M.M. described. Her *after* can only be truly appreciated if you know the amount of pounding rains she endured before she saw the first spiritual flower. Cathie's childhood years through her early twenties are marked by her inability to read. This challenge proved to be an irritant that provoked impatience, anger, and displeasure in her. Family struggles often took center stage, allowing her to hide her reading struggles. And hide them, she did. All the way through high school graduation. Given a chance to escape poverty and the dismal opportunities after high school, she swapped her ASVAB test with a friend, hoping his intelligent answers would allow her to join the military.

Her plan worked until she took the basic literacy exam during boot camp. When she couldn't read the questions, her secret was exposed. Getting kicked out of the Army became a real possibility. "In an attempt to stay, I volunteered for every 'hands-on' job: weapons specialist, motor pool, and fitness instructor.

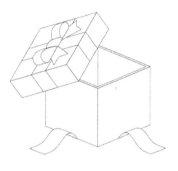

Those jobs involved some reading, but the pictorial language used in the military allowed me to get by. I knew I had to make myself valuable and useful." Several years later, a broken relationship combined with a continued struggle to learn to read led to a suicide attempt. Thankfully, she was unsuccessful. A friend invited her to church, and she met Jesus. "Accepting Christ as my Savior changed the trajectory of my life," Cathie shared.

Re-enlisting after her four years of duty wasn't an option because of her limited reading skills. Instead, Cathie enrolled in remedial reading classes at a local college. She and Jeff, the young man who prayed with her when she accepted Jesus, began dating. On a road trip, he learned Cathie couldn't help him navigate toward their destination. In a moment of bravery, she confessed she couldn't read the road signs. Instead of ridiculing her or embarrassing her, Jeff offered compassion and a desire to help her learn to read.

"I feel like God has called me to be here for you," Jeff told her. Six months later, Jeff and Cathie were married. She joined him in Boston where she continued her remedial classes. Jeff read books with her every night and consistently reminded her they were in this together. Several years later, psycho-educational testing led to diagnoses of dyslexia, dysgraphia, and ADHD. "For the first time in my life, I didn't feel stupid. Those diagnoses explained why I struggled to read, write, spell, and stay focused."

A FULL CIRCLE MOMENT

Cathie's determination, drive, and hard work opened the door for her to become a full-time student, taking regular college classes. While she worked to earn an associate degree in criminal justice, God was growing the gifts of courage and confidence in her. Literacy became a gift that no one could ever take away from her. Springing up beneath the pounding rains of illiteracy were the beautiful flowers of a bachelor's degree and a master's degree.

When Cathie reflected on all she'd overcome, she realized she felt a deep connection with students who struggle to read and write. A connection she could not ignore. Earning a special education teaching certificate became a full circle moment. Cathie still gets teary-eyed when she talks about her passion to help a multitude of students to learn to read and write. She embodies her purpose with the greatest energy and excitement of any teacher I know.

For several years, Cathie poured her heart into teaching kids who not only needed to learn to read and write, but who also needed a hero who'd been in their shoes. Brain research captured her interest, so Cathie worked toward and earned an Education Specialist degree, which allowed her to step into a school administrator role. Working in a Title 1 school for years as an assistant administrator widened the scope of students she could impact. She believes, "You don't overcome for you. You overcome, so you can impact others."

Two years ago, Cathie was named principal at a local elementary school. Equipping and empowering the teachers to improve the students' reading skills was her top priority. At the end of the 2022-2023 school year, the England Language Program, a national program that supports second language learners, recognized and awarded Cathie and the faculty at her school for increasing their students' English vocabulary by sixty-five percent. Isn't that a gorgeous flower?

NOTICE THE GIFTS AND BLESSINGS

Oh, how I pray you begin noticing or have been reminded to notice the gifts and blessings along the difficult parts of your journey. God desires for you to see these treasures to remind you He is with you, He is fighting for you, He hears your prayers and is acting, and He loves you with an unfailing love. Enjoy the beauty of those spiritual flowers. Thank God for sending them after the pounding rains.

Soak in the beauty of the waterfall one last time. To ensure your gift box doesn't get crushed, attach it to your carabiner and then to the outside of your backpack. It's time to keep moving forward!

We are all naturally seekers of wonders. We travel far to see the majesty of old ruins, the venerable forms of the hoary mountains, great waterfalls, and galleries of art. And yet the world's wonder is all around us; the wonder of setting suns, and evening stars, of the magic springtime, the blossoming of the trees, the strange transformations of the moth.[7]

—Albert Pike, Confederate States Army general

mile 16

Do You Spend Time Reflecting on Your Growth?

The real man (woman) smiles in trouble, gathers strength from distress, and grows brave by reflection.1

—Thomas Paine, founding father of America

H igh five, friend! You made it to the last mile of our journey! Making it here is no small feat. Before we begin hiking this mile, I wanted to share a few things with you. Throughout our journey together, I've been observing you.

You might not have noticed, but your countenance has changed. Long gone is the look of overwhelm. Instead, I see assurance and determination in your eyes. The worry crease on your forehead is fading. God's peace that surpasses all understanding has been filling you for weeks. When we first hit the trail, the weight of your challenges often caused you to stumble. Now, you stand tall, are prepared, and have the stamina required to face any challenge that intersects your path. May I point out one more noticeable change? God looks good IN you.

We use mirrors to reflect our image when putting on makeup, fixing our hair, and making sure a piece of salad from lunch isn't in our teeth. But mirrors are useful for so much more!

Time spent reflecting on your growth is a wise practice. Reflecting on who you've become and all you've learned may be the hardest part of our journey together. Throughout this mile, I invite you to see all the ways you've changed. How you've grown. And the areas of your life where you have room to grow even more. The visual image of a mirror will represent time spent reflecting on your growth.

Please mark your spot and find a mirror. Stare at your reflection for a few minutes. Think about your current challenge or a previous challenge.

Please don't rush this exercise. Think about the person you are now. Journal your answers to these questions: Who do you see? How did your challenge(s) impact you? What's changed in you? How do you view life differently?

REQUIRES BRAVERY

Thomas Paine's quote at the beginning of this mile states we grow "brave by reflection." *Merriam-Webster* defines *reflect* as "to make manifest or apparent; to show; to realize; to consider; to think quietly and calmly." Uh oh. Sounds like *introspection*, which *Merriam-Webster* defines as "a reflective looking inward; an examination of one's own thoughts and feelings." Looking inward? Examining our thoughts and feelings? No wonder Thomas Paine said we grow brave when we spend time reflecting.

Reflecting does require bravery. *Merriam-Webster* defines *bravery* as "having or showing mental and moral strength to face danger, fear, or difficulty; having courage." Looking back and examining your thoughts and feelings about the hardest times of your life does indeed take moral and mental strength. And courage!

Please consider the following precautions when you spend time reflecting. Sometimes when we reflect, we remember selectively. If you only remember the ways you royally messed up, failed, or hurt someone, you will become frustrated. Even angry. You might want to 'beat yourself up' for not heeding the warning signs. Shame will rear its ugly head and try to throw its burdensome cloak on you again. If you get tangled up in these thoughts and feelings, you will be tempted to throw your mirror on the ground and stomp on it. Shattering it into a million pieces.

Instead, you must also choose to remember how during those challenges you spent time comforting a friend who lost her job. You sent a gift card and words of encouragement to your child's teacher. And you entertained and made dinner for your neighbor's three young kids while she enjoyed shopping at the grocery store all by herself. Don't forget the gifts God scattered along your path: an unexplainable peace in the middle of the chaos, a skill you developed years ago became a skill you needed in your new job, and a new friend shared encouragement you didn't know you desperately needed.

LOOK AT GOD

Be careful to avoid the following two temptations. Perhaps you remember how you didn't need any pain medicine after your major surgery, which made you think of a coworker who ate painkillers like candy after her minor surgery. Comparisons like that will puff up your pride. King Solomon warned, "Pride goes before destruction, a haughty spirit before a fall" (Proverbs 16:18).

Maybe you remember problem-solving your challenge, taking action, and seeing positive outcomes—all before you even thought of trusting God with it. Likely, the enemy hissed in your ear, "See, you don't need God. You can handle challenges without Him." Putting confidence in your abilities, talents, connections, etc. is putting confidence in the wrong person. Through the prophet Jeremiah, the LORD said, "Cursed is the one who trusts in man ... But blessed is the one who trusts in the LORD, whose confidence is in him" (Jeremiah 17:5, 7).

The best way to avoid the temptations of being prideful and trusting in yourself is to notice all the ways God was with you during your challenges and worked them for your good. You might not have noticed them then, but now that you are taking the time to reflect, I believe you will be filled with awe. An awe that shouts, "Look at God!"

Look in your mirror again. A brave warrior is staring back at you. Do you see her? She is beautiful. Do you see him? He is handsome.

List the 'look at God!' awe you see when you reflect on your journey.

SEEING-THROUGH-TO-GOD PLACES

A quote from Ann Voskamp's book, *One Thousand Gifts*, caught my breath the first time I read it. She wrote, "I wonder too ... if the rent in the canvas of our life backdrop, the losses that puncture our world, our own emptiness, might actually become places to see. To see through to God. That which tears open our souls, those holes that splatter our sight, may actually become the thin, open places to see through the mess of this place to the heart-aching beauty beyond. To Him. To the God we endlessly crave. Maybe so. But how? How do we choose to allow the holes to become seeing-through-to-God places?" [2] Her words rolled around in my head for weeks. I understood them intellectually, but my heart struggled to process their significance.

Please highlight *losses that puncture our world, emptiness, tears open our souls, holes that splatter our sight,* **and** *mess of this place.*

Use a different color highlighter to highlight every instance of *see, sight,* **and** *seeing-through* **in the previous paragraph.**

Continue highlighting *see, sight, and seeing-through* **through the end of this mile. Additionally, highlight** *lost sight of and opened our eyes.*

Ann declared, "the losses that puncture our world, our own emptiness, might actually become places to see. To see through to God." The challenges that intersect our path can be losses that puncture our world and leave us feeling empty. Oh, how you and I long to see God working in our difficult circumstances. To look at His face and be reassured He's there and He's not leaving. Just to see His Presence, which would be a tangible reminder that He's with you.

Can you relate to Ann's other descriptions of places that allow us to see God: "that which tears open our souls, those holes that splatter our sight" and "the mess of this place"? Has a broken relationship torn open your soul? How about a wayward child's actions splattering your sight? Ann believes these challenges open our eyes to see "the heart-aching beauty beyond." The beauty beyond is God. It's hard to wrap our minds around it, but the goodness of God, the faithfulness of God, and the mercy of God can best be seen during our hard times.

SEE GOD'S GLORY

We are not alone in wanting to see God. Moses did too. Moses asked God to teach him and guide him as he led the Israelites to the Promised Land. The LORD replied, "My Presence will go with you" (Exodus 33:14). Imagine the reassurance Moses felt when God promised His Presence would go with them. God makes the same promise to you.

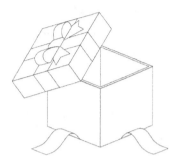

Describe how God's Presence going with you is a gift.

Even though God promised to go with the Israelites, Moses dared to ask one more thing. He asked to see God's glory (Exodus 33:18). God responded, "I will cause all my goodness to pass in front of you, and I will proclaim my name, the LORD, in your presence. I will have mercy on whom I will have mercy, and I will have compassion on whom I will have compassion. But you cannot see my face, for no one may see me and live" (Exodus 33:19-20).

Moses' request was bold. You can't blame him for asking. A person's face reveals as much, if not more, than his or her words. Couldn't we learn more about God if we could just see His face? We can see God, in ways which don't require our eyes. When you felt comforted during your deep grief, your eyes saw Jehovah Shammah, the Lord who is there. Maybe an unwanted divorce devastated your life and finances.

However, each month when you looked at the money in your account, you realized you could pay your bills and expenses. You saw Jehovah Jireh, the Lord who provides.

Perhaps you saw Jehovah Gibbor—the LORD the mighty warrior—fight for you when you were wrongly accused. When the not guilty verdict was given, you saw how He fought to maintain your good name. Our sinful choices separated us from God. When we accepted Jesus' forgiveness and salvation, we saw our Redeemer. Each of His names invites us to experience His character and see God beyond what our physical eyes can see.

How have you seen God? Describe how your challenges became "holes to seeing-through-to-God places."

CHANGE HOW I LIVE WITH IT

To an outsider looking in, Josie's ^{P} over-the-top positive attitude may look a bit Pollyanna-like. Please let me assure you, her big smile and positive affirmations are genuine. You'd expect someone living with a chronic illness to feel life is a never-ending cycle of suffering and exhaustion. But that's not how Josie feels. Freedom is what she feels. She believes, "The most important thing for me to focus on when I don't feel well is my relationship with God. I can't dwell on the pain and weariness. There is freedom in releasing that. My mindset might not change my illness, but it will change how I live with it."

Josie's chronic health struggles began in childhood. Despite multiple tests over the years, a diagnosis of chronic Lyme disease wasn't given until she was thirty-two years old. Effective treatments would surely follow now that she finally had a diagnosis and a name for her struggles, right? Not exactly. Years of painful and energy-draining treatments have helped, but they haven't been completely effective in ridding her body of the toxins of Lyme disease.

"It's all about removing the toxins that have built up in my body over time," Josie shared. "It's like a room that has been painted twenty times. My treatments are slowly removing layers of paint (toxins). As each layer is peeled away through detox, I experience—to a lesser degree—the same symptoms I was experiencing at the time that layer was painted. As crazy as it sounds, the pain from detox becomes a layer of healing."

After her treatments, Josie posts updates on her Facebook page, detailing how she sees-through-to-God in the hard places of her journey. One such post read, "Sometimes the good, the bad, and the ugly happen at the same moment. Sometimes the highs and lows are intertwined. Sometimes our spirits soar while our bodies crash. It's times like these when I feel God's presence deeply and intimately. I know that He is with me, guiding my life, and encouraging my heart even in the midst of suffering. He hasn't abandoned me. In fact, He's showing me that I'm right on track with the good plan He has for my life."

GOD SEES ME

Josie's social life is limited. The unexpected ways her body behaves makes going out risky. So, she considers dressing up and hanging out with friends a gift. Upon returning from a night out, she posted this on her social media: "I am so thankful for that special gift of a few good hours. It reminded me that God sees me, and He cares. God sees you too, and He cares what you are going through. This was a big gift, but there are little gifts every day. We just need to look for them. There are those little moments when you see something beautiful, and you're reminded that God made that."

Instead of anger toward God for allowing her illness to continue, Josie diligently maintains a positive outlook on life and an abiding trust in God. She believes God has been progressively transforming her into His image. Knowing she's looking more and more like Jesus fills her with confidence to pursue the passions God put in her heart.

In 2012, Josie became Vice President of the 'Broken but Priceless' ministry with her friend, Erin (from mile 07 in *Challenges Won't Stop Me*). Their mission is to help, support, and encourage those who live with chronic illnesses. Josie's award-winning book, *Howie's Broken Hee-Haw*, encourages children to see themselves as unique and of great value rather than broken. Because of the great love shown for Howie, Josie is writing a 90-day children's devotional titled *Howie and Friends*, which is scheduled to release in the summer of 2024.

DOT-TO-DOT PUZZLES

I'm revealing my age when I share how much I loved completing dot-to-dot puzzles when I was a kid. On Saturday mornings while watching cartoons, I completed numerous dot-to-dot puzzles at the coffee table in our den. Anticipation of what the completed picture would look like grew as I connected each dot.

Likewise, each piece of a jigsaw puzzle placed correctly is necessary to see the completed image. How about the cross-stitch piece with overlapping and knotted threads in mile 14? Each of those messy threads on the back side of the cross-stitch piece were necessary to see the gorgeous picture on the front.

Recently, I spent some time reflecting on my journey. I wanted to create a visual representation of what I was gaining from my reflection time, so I created a Dot-to-Dot. The large dots represented all the uphill chal-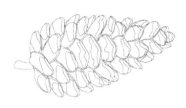lenges, refining fires, and snakes which have intersected my path. While pain, loss, frustration, grief, disappointment, and anxiety accompanied those difficult parts of my journey, spending time in reflection allowed me to see how each large dot was necessary to transform me into God's image.

Sadly, I realized some of the gifts and blessings God scattered along my path had gone unnoticed. I decided small dots would represent those gifts, such as my interests, job changes, and meeting people at just the right time. Seeing how the large dots (challenges) often led to the small dots (gifts) filled me with an abundance of gratitude.

When I finished my Dot-to-Dot reflection, I laid the two pages side-by-side. Wow! Seeing my journey in that format gave me a new perspective. I saw how all those uphill challenges, refining fires, and snakes transformed me, scraped off impurities which were limiting me, and acted as a fertilizer. My growth was undeniable. Look at God! I am in awe of God's work in my life.

My completed Dot-to-Dot Reflection looks quite different than the childhood dot-to-dot puzzles I completed. Mine looks more like a mind map, but I'm counting on you to 'get the picture.' Please allow my two-part Dot-to-Dot Reflection to encourage you to start thinking about the large and small dots in your journey. I'll invite you to create your own Dot-to-Dot Reflection near the end of this mile.

Melony's Dot-to-Dot Reflection, part 1

At two years old, a stroke attacked my brain and body. It caused residual deficits with the fine motor skills in my left hand, balance, coordination, reading comprehension, and word retrieval.

My parents encouraged me to try everything other kids did. I played sports and learned to ride a bike. Both activities strengthened my left side. My mom and dad's mindset of not allowing that stroke to define me or defeat me were the seeds of my 'challenges won't stop me' mindset.

The determination, perseverance, and grit I developed throughout my childhood fortified me to fight to overcome the learning challenges I faced in college.

I pursued a degree in special education, which required me to learn 'out-of-the-box' strategies to help students who struggle academically and behaviorally. Those strategies also helped me.

My limitations frustrated me, which led to learning different ways of participating in life. Devising my own style of typing would become a gift when God called me to write.

The residual challenges my stroke caused led to a deep compassion for others who struggle. Encouraging, equipping, and empowering anyone who is facing a challenge with the strategies, habits, and mindsets I've learned about fighting to overcome fills me with great joy.

The study strategies I relied on in high school weren't effective in college. Earning a D in English 101 sucker-punched my confidence. I feared my childhood neurologist's predictions about high school graduation being my ceiling were being fulfilled. The enemy tried to convince me that my dreams of becoming a teacher would not be realized because of my limitations.

I understand and can empathize with students who struggle academically. When I explain how my struggles led to discovering the strategies I share with them, my students are eager to try them. I've been blessed by their success stories throughout my teaching career.

Melony's Dot-to-Dot Reflection, part 2

At the high school where I wanted to work, teaching English was the only position available. I preferred teaching Math, but I took the job anyway. Almost daily, the enemy whispered, "You can't handle high school students" and "You can't teach English when reading comprehension is one of your biggest challenges."

Learning to annotate as I read significantly strengthened my reading comprehension skills. Teaching high school English increased my knowledge of and abilities with grammar, writing, editing, and revising.

Annotating novels, writing, revising, and editing are the skills the students I tutor need the most. These skills are integral when writing blogs and books.

My husband, Jeff, is by far the best gift God has given me. God knew I would need his compassion, care, encouragement, and love for the BIG challenges which began in my late 20s and will continue throughout my life.

I believed God could heal me, but He didn't. The refining fires taught me He would provide the strength I needed for each day. During those dark days, I felt His Presence and His comfort.

The refining fires of frequent and debilitating migraines tested me beyond what I thought I could endure. Initially, anger and frustration reigned. I missed many activities with Jeff and our sons. I also burned through all my allotted sick days at work.

A few months before turning 40, mini strokes began attacking me. Fears about having a stroke which would kill me or make me a burden to my family invaded my daily life and my dreams.

An angiogram of my brain revealed a rare, progressive neurological condition called Moyamoya disease. It was determined the best treatment to stop or slow the progression of this disease was brain surgery.

At the school where I taught, the faculty and staff supported me and my family in a myriad of ways: listening when I needed to vent about feeling weary, encouraging me to keep fighting to overcome, and praying for my healing. Their love and generosity continued throughout my brain surgery recovery, including donating their sick days, so I could continue earning income during my medical leave of absence.

While brain surgery is by far the biggest challenge to intersect my path, it also proved to be a gift. In a dozen ways, God revealed He would fulfill His promises to be with me, to fight for me, to protect me, and to surround me with His unfailing love.

AGENTS OF TRANSFORMATION

Throughout *Challenges Won't Stop Me* and *Keep Moving Forward*, I've shared stories of men and women in the Bible and snippets of stories from some of the overcomers I've interviewed. All those stories point to the truth that you are not alone in your challenges. We see how the challenges they faced impacted their lives. We see God didn't ignore their cries for help, abandon them, or tell them to figure it out on their own. It would seem their challenges initiated their transformations.

Merriam-Webster defines *transform* as "to change in composition or structure; to change the outward form or appearance of, to change in character or condition." Another word for transformation is *metamorphosis*, which *Merriam-Webster* defines as "a change in physical form, structure, or substance, especially by supernatural means; a striking alteration in appearance, character, or circumstances."

Did you notice the word *change* appears several times in both definitions? Few of us like change because change is hard. Change is exhausting. Change forces us outside our comfort zone. And change requires us to learn new skills or habits. Trust the changes you go through will be for your good. Those changes will cause a "striking alteration in your character." The outcome of your transformation? You will look more like Jesus.

PROTEIN SOUP

Remember studying the caterpillar to butterfly metamorphosis in middle school science? We are going to study it again. And this time, we are examining the nitty-gritty, slimy details.

As you read the phases of the butterfly's metamorphosis, mark challenges with a double underline and highlight any gifts.

Likely, you know a butterfly's life begins as a caterpillar. After hatching from an egg, the tiny caterpillar, or larva, begins gorging on leaves. These nutrient-rich leaves fill her with energy for the next phase of transformation.

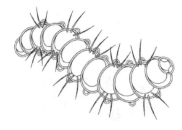

Transformation begins at birth—a bringing forth; a beginning. Describe how knowing your challenge is bringing forth a new beginning impacts you.

During your transformation, what did you gorge on? Was it junk or nutrient-rich? If you gorged on God's Word, describe how it filled you with energy for the next phase of transformation.

As the caterpillar grows, it no longer fits in its skin. The process of molting—shedding or casting off—the outer skin begins. Casting off sound familiar? During the refining process, dross—those people, activities, or habits holding you back—are cast off.

When that challenge intersected your path, do you remember feeling you no longer fit? List several adjectives which capture your thoughts and feelings during that time.

The caterpillar then suspends itself from a leaf and slides into its chrysalis. This time of tremendous change marks the beginning of the pupa stage. Inside the chrysalis, enzymes are released, which rip apart the caterpillar's muscles, digestive system, and other organs. Those cells dissolve and liquify into a goo, or protein soup. Specialized cells, containing the genetic recipe to form different body parts, begin forming the body of the adult butterfly.

Describe how your life was turned upside down and ripped apart during your transformation.

Perhaps the caterpillar becoming protein soup while in the chrysalis resonates with you. You remember numerous changes occurring all at once, leaving you a gooey mess. You didn't recognize it at first, but the huge shot of protein floating in your gooey mess kept your head above water. You needed protein, an important building block, for repairing things in your life 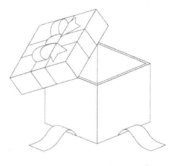 which weren't working properly, oxygenating/breathing new life into you, and regulating/bringing specific parts of your life under control.

Describe how you experienced repairing, oxygenating, and regulating during your time in the chrysalis.

WASTE STRENGTHENS

The hard, outer shell of the chrysalis protects the goo/protein soup from insects or birds harming or eating it. Time spent in the chrysalis varies between six to twelve days, depending on the type of butterfly. The butterfly's adult body is nearly complete.

Describe the protection you received when you were in the goo/protein soup.

Hormones are released into the chrysalis to soften the hard protective shell. While the hormones help soften the chrysalis, the adult butterfly must still wrestle to break through its temporary home. Meconium—waste produced during the pupal stage—coats the butterfly's wings, strengthening its wings for flight.

Meconium, or waste, strengthens a butterfly's wings for flight. List your takeaways.

When the pupal stage is complete, it's time for the butterfly to emerge. Breaking free presents a new challenge. An outside source breaking open the chrysalis harms, rather than helps, the butterfly. The transformed caterpillar pushes out of the chrysalis, ready to take flight as a beautiful butterfly.

Describe how pushing strengthens and develops you to take flight as a transformed creation.

A FORWARD OR ONWARD MOVEMENT

The apostle Paul described the process of transformation in 2 Corinthians 3:18. Notice his reference to seeing in a mirror. This verse reads, "And we all, with unveiled face, continually seeing as in a mirror the glory of the Lord, are progressively being transformed into His image from [one degree of] glory to [even more] glory, which comes from the Lord, [who is] the Spirit" (AMP).

None of us will be fully transformed until we see Jesus face-to-face. As Paul said, we are being progressively transformed. The root word of progressively is *progress*, which *Merriam-Webster* defines as "a forward or onward movement; advancing; gradual betterment; to develop to a higher, better, or more advanced stage." Be thankful you aren't a butterfly who undergoes a one-and-done transformation. Instead, you will progress gradually and develop throughout your earthly life. With each transformation, God transforms your character, motivations, and actions to look like Him. His work in you has the potential to impact our world in ways you never could have imagined.

GIVE HIM ALL THE CREDIT

Let's look at one more powerful overcomer story before I invite you to complete your Dot-to-Dot Reflection. A minister and his wife adopted Mary [Q] at birth, giving her opportunities to learn about God in church. She knew of Jesus, but she didn't know Him. Watching her adoptive mom struggle with alcoholism filled her with rebellion instead of grace.

Mary began her alcohol and drug addiction at the tender age of twelve. "And I continued on that path for a long time. Until I was thirty-four years old," she shared. A turning point happened when Mary looked in the mirror. She didn't like what she saw. Addictions to alcohol and drugs, a failed marriage, and piles of shame for her years of poor decisions stared back at her. "I looked back and saw a trail of rubble behind me. I'd given everything else a chance to fill me. And they didn't. I knew I needed to give Jesus a chance."

Accepting Christ opened Mary's eyes to a completely different life. Her sins were forgiven and washed away, and her heart opened to knowing God. The Holy Spirit began changing her heart. "God used the music in me that I wasn't using for His glory, and He changed my direction. I give Him all the credit. He used it [music] to restore me," she shared. Twenty-one years have passed since Mary gave her life to Jesus. She boasts that alcohol and drugs no longer control her; her marriage is strong and healthy; and her children know and love Jesus. God gets all the credit for these blessings and gifts.

LOVES AND USES BROKEN PEOPLE

When I asked Mary to reflect on her journey and share what she's learned, she said, "I know God loves and uses broken people. He takes their trials and issues and struggles and turns them around. That's where His power shows up."

Mary's reference of Paul's words in 2 Corinthians 12:9 reads, "But he said to me, 'My grace is sufficient for you, for my power is made perfect in weakness.' Therefore I will boast all the more gladly about my weaknesses, so that Christ's power may rest on me." Mary cannot boast in all she's done to turn things around in her life. She didn't do it. God did. And Mary does indeed boast in God, the One who restored her life. Through His transforming power in her, she impacts hundreds of thousands of lives with her music.

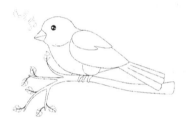

While Mary is a six-time Inspirational Country Music Female Vocalist of the Year, she will be the first to tell you those accolades are gifts and blessings pointing to God's transformative power in her life. Mary's heartfelt desire is for her music to give hope to all believers, especially broken people. Mary and her husband travel across the United States in their motor home to lead worship and share Bible-based messages with the hopes of inviting people into a deeper relationship with God. Experience Mary's beautiful music at mary jamesministries.org.

YOUR DOT-TO-DOT REFLECTION

Now, it is time to create your dot-to-dot reflection. Please do not skip this activity. You wouldn't have traveled this far to stop now, would you? Your dot-to-dot reflection will allow you to see how God has, is currently, and will continue to transform you from one degree of glory to even more glory. While you won't understand the purpose of every challenge, loss, pain, or failure you've faced, connecting the dots will reveal truths and growth you may not have been aware of.

Remember, large dots represent the uphill challenges, refining fires, and snakes you've faced. The small dots represent the gifts and blessings God scattered along the difficult parts of your path. Allow this exercise of reflection to be a seeing-through-to God.

As you begin, be reminded of Thomas Paine's words: We "grow brave by reflection." Be brave, my friend.

_____'s Dot-to-Dot Reflection, part 1

_____'s Dot-to-Dot Reflection, part 2

In what ways did this reflective exercise impact you?

Describe one or more of God's transformations that you now see because of time spent reflecting on your journey.

Where do you see instances of growth? Draw a tree beside those!

REFLECT OFTEN

Reflection is a powerful exercise. One which isn't limited to this dot-to-dot reflection. Take time to reflect often. When you do, you'll see God changing you through His Word, through your challenges, and through His unfailing love. He is transforming you to look like Him. Be encouraged by all the ways you see God working in your life. He is for you.

A blank dot-to-dot reflection sheet can be found at the back of this book. Make as many copies as you need to continue documenting the large and small dots in your life. If you feel led to share your Dot-To-Dot Reflection, I would be honored. You may email your reflections to reader7writer@gmail.com. Unless you grant permission, your reflection pages will not be shared.

It's almost time to say our goodbyes. But first, put a mirror in your backpack to remind you to reflect. I cannot wait to share a letter with you on the shuttle ride back to our cars.

Reflective thinking turns experience into insight.3

—Author, motivational speaker, and pastor, John C. Maxwell

KEEP MOVING FORWARD

Life is about accepting the challenges along the way, choosing to keep
moving forward, and savoring the journey.1

—Roy T. Bennett, author

A s we exited the trail, I expected to hear Sammy's lively greeting, inviting us to join him on the Shiny Shuttle. I scanned the entire parking lot. Sammy's shuttle bus was nowhere in sight. Neither was he.

I dropped my backpack on the ground and pulled out my phone. A ten percent battery warning popped up. I quickly typed Sammy a text message and sent it.

ME: Hey! Are you on your way?

SAMMY: Sadly, my shiny shuttle is sputtering and stammering. She's in the shop.

ME: I'm sorry your shuttle is in the shop, but your alliteration skills are top-notch today! Any ideas about how to get all my companions back to their cars? I can't ask them to backtrack eight miles. And we are exhausted and hungry.

SAMMY: Not to worry, Mel. I'm on it. I messaged the local school superintendent about borrowing a school bus. He was happy to help. ETA 2 hours.

ME: Thanks, Sammy. You ROCK!

GROWS DEEPER AND STRONGER

I headed over to the picnic table where everyone had gathered. When I delivered the news about our unexpected delay, several in our group groaned. The rest remained in good spirits. "Mind if I share the letter I was planning to read on our shuttle ride?"

No one objected. So, I continued, "Remember the Dear struggle letter from mile 02 in *Challenges Won't Stop Me*? I'll share a quick overview instead of reading it again. I pulled comments about the negative side of struggles from my notes on the overcomers I've interviewed. Then, I crafted the Dear Struggle letter with their heartfelt descriptions about how the challenges they faced negatively impacted their lives and all they felt they'd lost."

I held up the different Dear struggle I'd brought with me. "This Dear struggle letter flips the script. I read through my notes again to pull out what lessons those overcomers learned during their struggles. And how those challenges positively impacted their lives. In this letter, you'll hear their heartfelt descriptions about all they gained from their challenges."

Justin was seated to my left. I handed him copies of the Dear struggle letter and asked him to distribute them. Once everyone had a copy, I gave the following directions.

As you read the Dear struggle letter, underline phrases that resonate with you. Draw stars beside the lessons your challenges taught you. Highlight the gifts these overcomers discovered/gained.

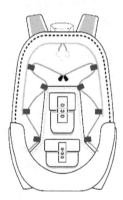

I ask you, my friend, to follow the same directions as you read the following Dear struggle letter.

Dear STRUGGLE,

I'm not the same person I was when I last wrote to you. I can bravely say hello, and it's good to know you. Because of you, what once was a gray story, is now a colorful story that brightens the lives of all those I share it with. Back then, I allowed you to convince me being stuck was my lot in life, but God showed me paths that lead to joy and an abundant life. Without the adversity you put in my path, I wouldn't have developed grit or perseverance. I used to beg God to take away my challenges. Now, I ask Him to show me their purpose. I've learned God's ways turn out far better than the ways I thought were best for my life. When despair threatened to crush me, His Word filled me with hope.

I've stumbled many times. I even thought giving up an easier road to take. But God equipped and empowered me to fight to overcome. When you darkened my path, I found God's light shining brightly. In your attempt to destroy me, God revealed His purpose and plan for my life. I declared Joseph's words: "You intended to harm me, but God intended it for good." I wouldn't have known this passion that now drives me if my path had been carefree and light. Instead of focusing on you, I fix my eyes on God and praise Him. God's armor defends me against every attack. When you put obstacles in my path, God has shown me that He is with me. The challenges you hoped would stop me were just opportunities to grow stronger. I seek God's hiding place when I need safety, protection, or rest. When enemies seek to bully or harm me, I know God is fighting for me.

➡

When a chronic illness invaded my body and God chose not to heal me, I trusted Him anyway. The times my pain felt overwhelming, I felt God's comfort and assurance. Experiencing God's comfort opened my eyes to people I can comfort and support during their struggles. Scraping off impurities in my life led to a level of pain I didn't think I could endure, but God saw dangers I couldn't see. I no longer listen to all the 'what if' scenarios filling my head. Those are lies from the enemy. Challenges are seeds that caused my faith to grow stronger and deeper roots. I discovered gifts and blessings are often hidden in my challenges. Praying invites me to give all my concerns to God. He hears me and lifts me close to Him. When I felt weary or hopeless, the love, support, and encouragement I received from friends and family reminded me how much we need each other.

When I reflected on my life, I realized how much you've taught me. The challenges I've fought to overcome are preparation for the challenges ahead. Every struggle I've encountered transformed me to look more and more like Jesus. No matter how many times you try to stop me, I will keep moving forward. I'm not just surviving. I'm thriving! Thank you for everything you've taught me.

Gratefully yours,

ME

I'm confident your challenges taught you other lessons. Add those below.

Dear struggle,

Gratefully,

If you already have a fight verse, write it here.

If you didn't start *Keep Moving Forward* with a fight verse, review the verses you highlighted throughout this book that were potential contenders. Narrow them down to one. Record your fight verse below.

Additionally, please write your fight verse in your Bible. And on several brightly colored index cards to put next to your bed, in the kitchen, in your purse or wallet, on your desk, and any other place you will see it.

RUGGED AND BUILT TO WITHSTAND

As you've created your two-part survival guide, you've discovered your essential gear is rugged and built to withstand whatever challenge dares to intersect your path. When you are blessed with weeks or months or years of minor challenges or no challenges, please don't store your gear in a dusty attic. Their power and effectiveness lie in consistently using them. These gifts equip and empower you to fight to overcome challenges AND to enjoy all the challenge-free and wonderfully ordinary days.

Oh, how God rejoices when you trust (lean on, rely on, and be confident in) this gear! I referred to and inserted the visual images of your essential gear throughout our journey together, expecting the repetition of these concepts to firmly stick in your head and heart. Let's test my theory.

Beside each piece of gear, write what it represents. Please attempt to complete this exercise from memory.

A pair of binoculars represents

A rope represents

A map represents

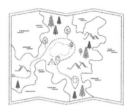

A travel log represents

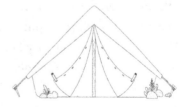

A tent represents

A multi-purpose tool represents

A flashlight represents

TO PLAN IN ADVANCE

We discovered the immense value of being prepared for the unexpected turns during our journey in *Challenges Won't Stop Me*. Preparing—to make ready beforehand; to put in a proper state of mind; to plan in advance—for encounters every person can expect and should expect is equally as valuable. As we journeyed together in *Keep Moving Forward*, each mile presented situations you can expect to encounter one or more times during your life. As before, I referred to and inserted visual images of the expected encounters throughout these eight miles, expecting the repetition of these concepts to firmly stick in your head and heart. Time to test my theory again.

Beside each expected encounter, write what it represents. Please attempt to complete this exercise from memory. But if you need your notes, please use them.

Two hikers represent

Hikers cannot fit in your backpack. Sunflowers can. They represent

A mirror represents

A tree does not fit in your backpack. So, acorns and leaves represent

A carabiner represents

Fire should not be put in your backpack. So, a box of matches represents

A first aid kit represents

Snakes represent

Please do not put a snake in your backpack! Instead, throw the number for Poison Control in there.

POISON
CONTROL
1-800-222-1222

A waterfall represents

Sadly, a waterfall won't fit in your backpack. But a gift box will!

How about some extra credit?

The caterpillar to a butterfly represents

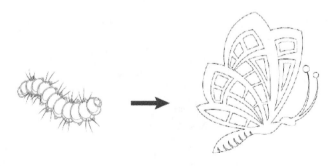

A trail sign represents

A rainbow represents

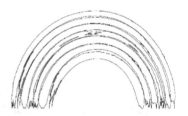

Fill in the missing words. To check your answers, refer back to page 29.

For easy reference, please label a sticky note with **VISUAL IMAGES.** Now, add it to the edge of the page where you wrote what a pair of binoculars represents.

FORWARD MOVEMENT

How did you do? I imagine you knew all or most of the visual images and what they represent. Surprised? I'm not. Researchers at Michigan State University discovered, "Images can strongly influence the way we act. Because we process visual stimulation at lightning speed, images are likely to prompt strong emotion, which in turn can lead to action." [2]

Ah, action! Yes, isn't action just forward movement? My prayer is you will recall or come back to these pages to remind you to not let the challenges of life stop you. You will use your gear to fight to overcome.

You will look for God's hand in your challenges. You will trust how He is transforming you during challenges and during life's expected encounters. And you will actively and with purpose keep moving forward!

In the RESTED, RECHARGED & READY introduction, Hugh shared this wisdom: "Challenges are just cleverly disguised opportunities to grow."

Now that you've walked these miles of expected encounters, record your thoughts and feelings about Hugh's words.

YOUR DESTINY AND YOUR ETERNAL HOME

This challenging and beautiful journey through life IS about finding the "seeing-through-to-God" places as Ann Voskamp described. I trust you are seeing-through to how God repurposes every challenge that intersects your path all while transforming you for what lies ahead: your destiny and your eternal home with God.

Your destiny is the 'thing' God made YOU for. It's the unique way you can and will impact lives. Like no other person. When you impact lives, you are glorifying God. Ephesians 2:10 reminds us, "we are God's handiwork, created in Christ Jesus to do good works, which God prepared in advance for us to do." God equipped YOU for specific good works.

And living out YOUR good works will be the very 'thing' others need.

All you've learned from your challenges and all the gifts you've been given on your journey of overcoming will benefit, encourage, and inspire others. They will see God through YOU! Your life will point them to Him, the One who loves and forgives and desires to save them. And when God calls you away from the troubles of this world, your eternal home awaits you!

CONQUERED IT FOR YOU

We read John 16:33 in mile 01 and in REST & RECHARGE in *Challenges Won't Stop Me*. Here, at the end of our journey, I wanted to share it again. In a discussion with His disciples about leaving this world and going to the Father, Jesus said, "I have told you these things, so that in Me you may have [perfect] peace and confidence.  In the world you have tribulation and trials and distress and frustration; but be of good cheer [take courage; be confident, certain, undaunted]! For I have overcome the world. [I have deprived it of power to harm you and have conquered it for you]" (John 16:33, AMPC).

A dozen or so verses prior to Jesus declaring we will have trouble in this world, He said, "I assure you, most solemnly I tell you, that you shall weep and grieve, but the world will rejoice. You will be sorrowful, but your sorrow will be turned into joy" (John 16:20, AMPC). While we will experience trouble and grief in this world, Jesus encouraged the disciples (and us) to look forward to the joy we will experience in seeing Him face-to-face in Heaven. We keep moving forward despite the trouble and grief in this world, knowing it's all pointing toward Him and our Heavenly home!

Hebrews 11, known as the Hall of Fame of Faith, describes the men and women who didn't run from challenges. Instead, knowing God was

204 | MELONY BROWN

with them, they fought to overcome those challenges. Their faith grew vigorously despite everything that was meant to defeat or destroy them. Among others mentioned in Hebrews 11, we learn Abraham's focus wasn't on the struggles ten feet in front of him. Quite the opposite: "For he was [waiting expectantly and confidently] looking forward to the city which has foundations, [an eternal, heavenly city] whose architect and builder is God" (Hebrews 11:10, AMPC). Abraham kept moving forward because he believed the ultimate outcome—Heaven—was worth every challenge, obstacle, trouble, and adversity he endured in this world.

As a declaration of your overcoming and thriving, please write the following two sentences in your own handwriting.

The challenges of this world won't stop me. I will keep moving forward because I know what I learn from each challenge is preparing me for my eternal home——Heaven!

CONTINUING, PERSISTANT FAITH

The apostle John wrote the prophetic book of Revelation. The twenty-two chapters of Revelation contain prophecy about the end times, which can feel both scary and hopeful. Mostly scary, right? I encourage you to find a far wiser person than me to help you understand the scary parts, but I am excited to share what I learned when I typed the word *overcome* into biblegateway.com.

As you read the following verses in the Amplified translation (AMP), highlight that which resonates with you and fills you with hope.

Revelation 2:7 "To him who overcomes [the world through believing that Jesus is the Son of God], I will grant [the privilege] to eat [the fruit] from the tree of life, which is in the Paradise of God."

Revelation 2:11 "He who overcomes [the world through believing that Jesus is the Son of God] will not be hurt by the second death (the lake of fire)."

Revelation 2:17 "To him who overcomes [the world through believing that Jesus is the Son of God], to him I will give [the privilege of eating] some of the hidden manna, and I will give him a white stone with a new name engraved on the stone which no one knows except the one who receives it."

Revelation 3:5 "He who overcomes [the world through believing that Jesus is the Son of God] will accordingly be dressed in white clothing; and I will never blot out his name from the Book of Life, and I

206 | MELONY BROWN

will confess and openly acknowledge his name before My Father and before His angels [saying that he is one of Mine]."

Revelation 31:7 "He who overcomes [the world by adhering faithfully to Christ Jesus as Lord and Savior] will inherit these things, and I will be his God and he will be My son."

Describe how these verses encourage you to "be of good cheer [take courage; be confident, certain, undaunted]" when you encounter "tribulation and trials and distress and frustration."

These verses are full of promises! Promises for those of us who believe Jesus is the Son of God and who abide faithfully in Him. The apostle Paul encourages you and me to fix our eyes on the prize: "I press on toward the goal to win the [heavenly] prize of the upward call of God in Christ Jesus" (Philippians 3:14). How do we press on? Say it with me, "We keep moving forward!"

GOD'S GREAT WORK IN YOUR LIFE

Friend, you did it! I'm so grateful you chose to invest your time in reading and completing this two-part interactive survival guide. What an honor to have journeyed with you! I pray all you gained will continue to remind you of God's great work in your life. May His favor and unfailing love cover you until you meet Jesus face-to-face.

Sammy honked several times to announce the battered and dirty school bus had arrived. He welcomed each weary traveler as they climbed the steps. Before I ascended the steps, I paused to thank God for all we learned throughout our sixteen-mile journey. I've loved seeing-through to the great work God's doing in and through you. And I'm humbled by the great work God has done in and through me. I must admit I'm just as weary as you are. Resting and recharging are definitely in my future. I hope in yours, too.

A trail sign, unlike the usual ones, caught my attention. It appeared homemade rather than mass produced. Etched into the wood were neither trail names nor mile markings. Instead, a simple arrow pointing forward offered guidance to all those who will pass by it. While it may be a simple arrow to some, we know it symbolizes far more.

It is finally time to part ways. I echo the apostle Paul's words: "There has never been the slightest doubt in my mind that the God who started this great work in you would keep at it and bring it to a flourishing finish on the very day Christ Jesus appears" (Philippians 1:6, AMPC).

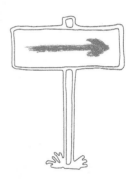

Until we meet again, may you continue to thrive and impact lives for God's kingdom!

"Sometimes in His provision for us, the Lord asks us to trust Him and move forward without having all the answers, to trust He will sustain us even in the things that feel like a mystery to us." 3

—Kristi McLelland, seminary professor and author

ANSWERS

From *RESTED, RECHARGED & READY*

- map
- binoculars
- tent
- multi-purpose tool
- rope
- travel log
- flashlight

_____'s Dot-to-Dot Reflection, part __

ACKNOWLEDGEMENTS

My village ROCKS! I am grateful for the following people who believe in me and the message of this book.

Thank you to ...

My overcomer family. Thank you for being my tribe. You get me. And I get you. You are precious gifts. When I reflect on the love and laughter I've enjoyed throughout the years of being friends with each of you, I am filled with gratitude.

My editor, Marcie Bridges. Thank you for your thoughtful revision suggestions and encouraging words throughout the editing process.

My proofreader, Cheryl Lutz. Add master proofreader to all the reasons I love you. Riding to CCC 2020 together led to a first-hand experience of C. S. Lewis' quote: "What! You too? I thought I was the only one." So grateful God intersected our paths! Your friendship is a blessing!

My interior designer, Catherine Posey. Thank you for creating an amazing interior design for my words. And for your incredible patience!

My book cover designer, Hannah Linder. Thank you for once again creating a beautiful cover. You have mad skills!

My rock star husband, Jeff Brown. Thank you for picking up Jimmy John sandwiches or REV Coffee blueberry hibiscus tea when my brain needed refueling. I love you! We make the best team.

My mother-in-law, Sandra Brown. Thank you for loving me like a daughter. You are one of the best of all God's gifts.

My aunts, Linda Smith and Carol Coleman. Your belief in me is both humbling and energizing. Thank you for your encouraging words and prayers over the years.

My best friend, Cathie Seibert. Only God could have orchestrated intersecting our lives in such a unique way. And I'm so grateful He did. Your zeal for life, your on-the-spot prayers, your hunger for time in nature, your love for God's Word, and your BIG hugs are but a few of the countless reasons I love you! Hawaii 2023! Please do some reconnaissance soon for our next adventure.

My God. Like Moses, I would not want to go on this journey without Your Presence. And just like you answered his request, you answered mine. Your Presence has been palpable. Your Word is indeed a powerful weapon when fighting spiritual warfare. I'm so grateful you entrust me to share the message of overcoming and thriving. May this book glorify you.

APPENDIX OF OVERCOMER STORIES

This appendix contains the location of each overcomer's story on my website, which may be accessed at melonybrown.com. Each overcomer listed below gave written permission to use a snippet of her story in this book.

A. Christine's Zigzag & 1 podcast interview—Season 4, episode 53— "An Invitation to Sit at His Table," 17 Feb. 2022, Podcast tab and Christine's Challenges Won't Stop Me podcast interview—Season 5, episode 79— "Joy Comes in the Morning," 22 Apr. 2023, Podcast tab.

B. Tiffany's Challenges Won't Stop Me podcast interview—Season 5, episode 78— "Drew Me Out of Deep Waters," 24 Mar. 2023, Podcast tab.

C. Lisa's Zigzag & 1 podcast interview—Season 1, episode 6— "Building Your Faith Muscle," 5 Apr. 2019, Podcast tab.

D. Zoe's story—To honor her request for privacy, no further information is available.

E. Addlia's story, "A Place to Call Home: The Flip Side of Homelessness," 30 Nov. 2018, Stories tab.

F. Emmie's story, "Get Busy Living," 22 Feb. 2018, Stories tab.

G. Alyssa's story, "Redeeming Love," 19 Jun. 2014, Stories tab.

H. Ruby's story, "Ruby Is a Gem," 21 Mar. 2017, Stories tab.

I. Aimee's story, "Front-Line Caregiver," 10 May 2018, Stories tab.

J. Niki's story, "Party of One," 4 Jun. 2015, Stories tab.

K. Teres'sa's story, "Warrior Woman: Hear My Cry," 11 Aug. 2016, Stories tab.

L. Tiffany's story, "Happiness Is a Choice," 29 Mar. 2018, Stories tab.

M. Dianne's story, "Grateful, Part 1," 29 Jun. 2017 and "Grateful, Part 2," 6 Jul. 2017, Stories tab.

N. Cathie's story, "Could No Longer Hide My Functional Illiteracy," 20 Sept. 2019, Stories tab.

O. Tamiko's Zigzag & 1 podcast interview—Season 3, episode 43— "Turning Pain into Purpose," 14 May 2021, Podcast tab.

P. Josie's story, "Freedom," 26 Apr. 2018, Stories tab.

Q. Mary's Zigzag & 1 podcast interview—Season 2, episode 26— "Music Is Restorative," 29 May 2020, Podcast tab.

NOTES

RESTED, RECHARGED & READY!

1. Simon, John D. "Address to the Class of 2019." University Convocation, 23 Aug. 2015, Lehigh University, Bethlehem, PA. Keynote Address.
2. King, Jr., Martin Luther. "Keep Moving from This Mountain." Founder's Day Address, 10 April 1960, Spelman College, Atlanta, GA. Keynote Address. www.kinginstitute. stanford.edu/king-papers/documents/keep-moving-mountain-address-Spelman-college- 10-april-1960.

mile 09: Will You Trust Your Connection to God?

1. Juma, Norbert, editor. "Praise God Quotes to Praise the Glory of God." Everyday Power, 8 Jan. 2023, www.everydaypower.com/praise-god-quotes.
2. Spurgeon, Charles H. The Complete Works of Charles Spurgeon, Volume 13: Sermons 728 to 787. Delmarva Publications, 2015, 91.
3. Ziglar, Tom. Foreword. Embrace the Struggle: Living Life on Life's Terms by Zig Ziglar and Julie Ziglar Norman, Howard Books, 2009, p. xi.

mile 10: Are You Growing and Thriving Despite Your Challenges?

1. McGill, Bryant (@Bryant McGill). "Let go. Life moves forward. The old leaves wither, die and fall away, and the new growth extends forward into the light. —Bryant McGill." 11 Nov. 2017. Facebook post.
2. Emerson, Ralph Waldo. Essays, First Series, produced by Tony Adam and David Widger, E-book, Project Gutenberg, 2021.
3. Fox, Maggie. "Nobel winner overcame personal loss, cancer, and being a woman." NBC News: Health News, 3 Oct. 2018, www.nbcnews.com/health/health-news/nobel-winner-overcame-personal-loss-cancer-being-woman-n916391. NCC Staff.

4. "Benjamin Franklin's last great quote and the Constitution." *National Constitution Center*, 13 Nov. 2022, www.constitutioncenter.org/blog/benjamin-franklins-last-great-quote-and-the-constitution.

5. Cisneros, Sandra. *The House on Mango Street.* Vintage Contemporaries, 1984, 75.

mile 11: Are Your Challenges Consuming You or Refining You?

1. "About Elliott, Elisabeth: Missionary to Ecuador, inspirational author, and worldwide speaker." Elisabethelliott, www.elisabethelliot.org/about.

2. Betram, Robin. *No Regrets: How Loving Deeply and Living Passionately Can Impact Your Legacy Forever.* Charisma House, 2017, 27.

mile 12: Who Is Journeying with You?

1. Voskamp, Ann. *The Broken Way: A Daring Path into the Abundant Life.* Zondervan, 2016, 173.

2. Dalton-Smith, Saundra. *Sacred Rest: Recover Your Life, Renew Your Energy, Restore Your Sanity.* FaithWords, 2017, 77.

3. Ibid., 78.

4. Ibid., 78.

5. Ibid., 78.

6. Ibid., 84.

7. McLelland, Kristi. *Jesus & Women: In the First Century and Now.* Lifeway Press, 2022, 14.

8. "The 60+ Best Winnie the Pooh Quotes." *Card Sayings,* www.cardsayings.net/best-winnie-the-pooh-quotes.

mile 13: Are Your Fear and Enemies Poisoning You?

1. Meyer, Joyce. "Fear Not!" *Joyce Meyer Ministries,* 5 May 2023, www.joycemeyer. org/dailydevo/2023/05/05-Fear-Not.

2. Lucado, Max. "Strongholds." *Words of Hope and Help,* Sept. 2015, www.maxlucado. com/strongholds.

3. Jones, Sam. "While Squeezing the Life out of Their Prey." *The New York Times,* 31 Mar. 2022, www.nytimes.com/2022/03/24/science/boa-constrictors- breathing.html#:~:text= With%20part%20of%20its%20-body,ribs%20to%20keep%20itself%20breathing.

4. Cahoon, Lauren. "Scorpions to Snakes; Bites and Stings That Hurt the Most." *ABC News,* 14 May 2009, www.abcnews.go.com/Health/PainManagement/story?id=7588073&page=1#:~:text=If%20there's%20a%20family%20of,from%20an%20African%20bush%20viper.

5. "Enemy Quotes That Will Make You Want to Cut Ties With Your Frenemies." *Everyday Power,* 9 Apr. 2023, www.everydaypower.com/enemy-quotes.

mile 14: How are You Treating Your Illnesses and Injuries?

1. Sodhi, Niharikaa Kaur. "7 Micro Perspectives to Help you Lead a Healthier Life." *Medium,* 2 Sept. 2021, www.medium.com/in-fitness-and-in-health/7-micro-perspectives-to-help-you-lead-a-healthier-life-164e1bbab4e2.

2. Aquinas, St. Thomas. "Commentary on the Gospel of St. John: Part I: Chapters 1-7," 707. Translated by James A. Weisheipl, O.P., Magi Books, Inc., New York, www.isidore.co/ aquinas/english/John5.htm.

3. Ibid, 710.

4. Ibid, 713.

5. Ibid, 716.

6. Bush, Sophia (@sophiabush). "You are allowed to be both a masterpiece and a work in progress, simultaneously. You are. #MondayMantra." 2 Nov. 2015. Tweet.

7. Nouwen, Henri J. *You Are the Beloved: Daily Meditations for Spiritual Living.* Convergent, 2017, 92.

mile 15: Have You Noticed the Gifts Scattered Throughout the Difficult Parts of Your Journey?

1. Keegan, Michael J. "On the Importance of Being Resilient." *IBM Center for the Business of Government*, 20 Jan. 2022, www.businessofgovernment.org/blog/importance-being-resilient.

2. Kloser, Christine. *A Daily Dose of Love: Everyday Inspiration to Help You Remember What Your Heart Already Knows*, Capucia Publishing, 2022, 24.

3. Halvorson, Heidi Grant. "The Science of Success: The If-Then Solution: No Willpower? No problem." *Psychology Today*, 21 Dec. 2020, www.psychologytoday.com/us/articles/ 201101/the-science-success-the-if-then-solution.

4. "Carlos Santana Quotes." *Quotefancy*, www.quotefancy.com/carlos-santana-quotes.

5. Mex, Friz (@Friz Mex). "Waterfalls wouldn't sound so melodious if there were no rocks in their way." 8 Oct. 2021. Pinterest pin.

6. Cowman, L.B. *Streams in the Desert: 366 Daily Devotional Readings*. Zondervan, 1997, 234.

7. Ahmad, Abdullah Saghir. "Every Landscape Tells a Story." *Medium*, 20 Apr. 2020, www.abdullahsaghirahmad.medium.com/every-landscape-tells-a-story-376a85c8abe2.

mile 16: Do You Spend Time Reflecting on Your Growth?

1. "Choose to be Brave and Fight for Your Dreams." *Be an Inspirer*, 20 June 2023, www.beaninspirer.com/choose-brave-fight-dreams.

2. Voskamp, Ann. *One Thousand Gifts: A Dare to Live Fully Right Where You Are*, Zondervan, 2010, 22.

3. "Reflect and Revise: A 5-Step Process for Personal Growth." *Maxwell Leadership*, 16 May 2023, www.maxwellleadership.com/blog/5-step-process-for-personal-growth.

KEEP MOVING FORWARD

1. Baldwin, AnnaGrace. "President's Letter: Challenge and Champion." *Nevada School Counselor Association*, 2019, March, www. schoolcounselor.org/Newsletters/April-2019/President%E2%80%99s-Letter-Challenge-and-Champion?st=NV.

2. "The psychology of visuals, how images impact decision making." *Enterprise The State of The Nation*, 5 Feb. 2020, www.enterprise.press/ stories/2020/02/05/the-psychology-of-visuals-how-images-impact-decision-making-11273.

3. McLelland, Kristi. *Jesus & Women: In the First Century and Now*, Lifeway Press, 2022, 45.

JOURNEY ON QUIZ

Fully trusting God and remaining joyful?
Anxiously wondering how you will make it?
Maintaining a flexible, easy-going attitude?
Confidently believing God is working?
Feeling discouraged and overwhelmed?

Take the twenty-question quiz at **journeyonquiz.com**
to discover which journey personality you are!

OUR EYES ARE
ON YOU, LORD
an interactive devotional

Journey On!
SERIES
BOOK 3

Vast armies came to wage war with Israel. King Jehoshaphat responded by inquiring of the LORD and praying, "We do not know what to do, but our eyes are on you."

Whether vast armies are coming against you, or sunshine and laughter abounds, responding as King Jehoshaphat did, directs your focus to the One who controls the universe. The One who lavishes you in His unfailing love. And the One who fights for you.

Our Eyes Are on You, the third book in Melony Brown's Journey On! series, offers a daily invitation to trust God with your frustratingly challenging days AND with your blissfully ordinary days. Grab a pen, highlighter, and colored pencils to actively engage with devotions geared to draw you closer to the One who holds your life and your future in His hands.

COMING SOON!

Printed in the USA
CPSIA information can be obtained
at www.ICGtesting.com
JSHW012249161123
52113JS00003B/5